Living Values™ Education

Living Values Education Activities for Children Ages 3–7, Book 1

DEVELOPED AND WRITTEN BY
Diane G. Tillman and Diana Hsu

WITH ADDITIONAL ACTIVITIES AND STORIES FROM
Dominique Ache
Encarnación Royo Costa
Dina Eidan
Tea Lobjanidze
John McConnel
Marcia Maria Lins de Medeiros
Max and Marcia Nass
Madeline C. Nella
Peter Williams
and other educators around the world

www.livingvalues.net

Tillman, Diane G.
     Living Values Education Activities for Children Ages 3–7, Book 1 / developed and written by
Diane G. Tillman with additional stories and activities from Dominique Ache . . . [et al].
     Includes bibliographical references
     ISBN: 9781731087775

This is an update and expansion of the 2000 original book, *Living Values Activities for Children Ages 3–7*, published by Health Communications, Inc. The expanded version has two volumes, Book 1 and Book 2, and is published independently by the Association for Living Values Education International (ALIVE), a non-profit Swiss Association, through Kindle Direct Publishing.

ALIVE Address: Rue Adrien-Lachenal 20, 1207 Genève, Switzerland
For information about professional development workshops and LVE generally, please visit ALIVE's website at www.livingvalues.net.

The development and advancement of Living Values Education is overseen by the **Association for Living Values Education International** (ALIVE), a non-profit-making association of organizations around the world concerned with values education. ALIVE groups together national bodies promoting the use of the Living Values Education Approach and is an independent organization that does not have any particular or exclusive religious, political or national affiliation or interest. The development and implementation of Living Values Education has been supported over the years by a number of organizations, including UNESCO, governmental bodies, foundations, community groups and individuals. LVE continues to be part of the global movement for a culture of peace following the United Nations International Decade for a Culture of Peace and Non-violence for the Children of the World.

Graphic design of cover by David Warrick Jones
Cover image of globe with children purchased from Shutterstock
Inside artwork for the "Lily the Leopard" and "The Happy Sponge" by Milk Aoyama, Japan
Inside artwork at the beginning of each values unit and several stories by I Wayan Agus Aristana, Media
     Productions, Karuna Bali Foundation, Ubud, Bali
Inside artwork for the "Rosa, David and the Tern" stories by Mary Monette Barbaso-Crall
Former editors: Carol Gill and Allison Janse

CONTRIBUTING ARTISTS

Milk Aoyama
I Wayan Agus Aristana
Mary Monette Barbaso-Crall

CONTENTS

Values Units . . .

Peace I . Respect I . Love and Caring . Tolerance . Honesty . Happiness
Responsibility . Simplicity and Caring for our Earth and Her Oceans

Unit Three: Love and Caring

Unit Six: Happiness

Unit Seven: Responsibility

Unit Eight: Simplicity and Caring for the Earth and her Oceans

Appendix

The Living Values Education Approach

After ten years of implementing Living Values Education, a team of LVE leaders around the world gathered together to describe what they felt LVE was … and had become.

Vision Statement

Living Values Education is a way of conceptualizing education that promotes the development of values-based learning communities and places the search for meaning and purpose at the heart of education. LVE emphasizes the worth and integrity of each person involved in the provision of education, in the home, school and community. In fostering quality education, LVE supports the overall development of the individual and a culture of positive values in each society and throughout the world, believing that education is a purposeful activity designed to help humanity flourish.

Core Principles

Living Values Education is based on the following core principles:

On the learning and teaching environment

1. When positive values and the search for meaning and purpose are placed at the heart of learning and teaching, education itself is valued.
2. Learning is especially enhanced when occurring within a values-based learning community, where values are imparted through quality teaching, and learners discern the consequences, for themselves, others and the world at large, of actions that are and are not based on values.
3. In making a values-based learning environment possible, educators not only require appropriate quality teacher education and ongoing professional development, they also need to be valued, nurtured and cared for within the learning community.
4. Within the values-based learning community, positive relationships develop out of the care that all involved have for each other.

On the teaching of values

5. The development of a values-based learning environment is an integral part of values education, not an optional extra.

6. Values education is not only a subject on the curriculum. Primarily it is pedagogy; an educational philosophy and practice that inspires and develops positive values in the classroom. Values-based teaching and guided reflection support the process of learning as a meaning-making process, contributing to the development of critical thinking, imagination, understanding, self-awareness, intrapersonal and interpersonal skills and consideration of others.

7. Effective values educators are aware of their own thoughts, feelings, attitudes and behavior and sensitive to the impact these have on others.

8. A first step in values education is for teachers to develop a clear and accurate perception of their own attitudes, behavior and emotional literacy as an aid to living their own values. They may then help themselves and encourage others to draw on the best of their own personal, cultural and social qualities, heritage and traditions.

On the nature of persons within the world and the discourse of education

9. Central to the Living Values Education concept of education is a view of persons as thinking, feeling, valuing whole human beings, culturally diverse and yet belonging to one world family. Education must therefore concern itself with the intellectual, emotional, spiritual and physical wellbeing of the individual.

10. The discourse of education, of thinking, feeling and valuing, is both analytic and poetic. Establishing a dialogue about values within the context of a values-based learning community facilitates an interpersonal, cross-cultural exchange on the importance and means of imparting values in education.

Structure

The development and advancement of Living Values Education is overseen by the **Association for Living Values Education International** (ALIVE), a non-profit-making association of organizations around the world concerned with values education. ALIVE groups together national bodies promoting the use of the Living Values Education Approach and is an independent organization that does not have any particular or exclusive religious, political or national affiliation or interest. The development and implementation of Living Values Education has been supported over the years by a number of organizations, including UNESCO, governmental bodies, foundations, community groups and individuals. LVE continues to be part of the global movement for a culture of peace following the United Nations International Decade for a Culture of Peace and Non-violence for the Children of the World.

ALIVE is registered as an association in Switzerland. In some countries national Living Values Education associations have been formed, usually comprised of educators, education officials, and representatives of organizations and agencies involved with student or parent education.

Activities

In pursuing its mission and implementing its core principles, the Association for Living Values Education International and its Associates and Focal Points for LVE provide:

1. *Professional development courses, seminars and workshops* for teachers and others involved in the provision of education.

2. *Classroom teaching material and other educational resources*, in particular an award-winning series of resource books containing practical values activities and a range of methods for use by educators, facilitators, parents and caregivers to help children and young adults explore and develop widely-shared human values. The original series of five books, now updated and expanded, plus Living Green Values and an additional 11 values-education resources for young people at risk, are specified in the following LVE Resource Materials section. The approach and lesson content are experiential, participatory and flexible, allowing — and encouraging — the materials to be adapted and supplemented according to varying cultural, social and other circumstances.

3. *Consultation to government bodies, organizations, schools, teachers and parents* on the creation of values-based learning environments and the teaching of values.

4. *An extensive website*, www.livingvalues.net, with materials available for downloading free of charge, including songs, posters and a distance program for adults, families and study groups.

LVE Resource Materials

Designed to address the whole child/person, Living Values Education Activities engage young people in exploring, experiencing and expressing values so they can find those that resonant in their heart, and build the social and emotional skills which enable them to live those values. The approach is child-centered, flexible and interactive; adults are asked to act as facilitators. The approach is non-prescriptive and allows materials and strategies to be introduced according to the circumstances and interests of the users and the needs of students.

The Living Values Education Series

The Living Values Education series, a set of five books first published in April of 2001 by Health Communications, Inc. (HCI), was awarded the 2002 Teachers' Choice Award, an award sponsored by *Learning* magazine, a national publication for teachers and educators in the USA. Materials from the books, and in some cases up to all five of the books, have been published in a dozen languages.

The original Living Values Education Series
♦ *Living Values Activities for Children Ages 3–7*
♦ *Living Values Activities for Children Ages 8–14*
♦ *Living Values Activities for Young Adults*
♦ *Living Values Parent Groups: A Facilitator Guide*
♦ *LVEP Educator Training Guide*

In 2018, the Association for Living Values Education International began updating this initial set of five books. Building on the original material, updated information, an expansion of activities and additional values units were added. Because of the amount of additional content, the original three Living Values Activities books are published by ALIVE as two volumes, Book 1 and Book 2. ALIVE's intent in separating from HCI, our esteemed publisher, was to make these educational resources more accessible to educators in all continents by offering the series not only as regular books but as eBooks and small free downloadable units.

The updated and expanded Living Values Education Series
♦ *Living Values Education Activities for Children Ages 3–7, Book 1*
♦ *Living Values Education Activities for Children Ages 3–7, Book 2*
♦ *Living Values Education Activities for Children Ages 8–14, Book 1*
♦ *Living Values Education Activities for Children Ages 8–14, Book 2*
♦ *Living Values Education Activities for Young Adults, Book 1*
♦ *Living Values Education Activities for Young Adults, Book 2*

from Brazil, Diana Hsu from Germany and Pilar Quera Colomina from Spain. As LVE spread to different countries and the books were translated into different languages, LVE educators in different countries added in their own cultural stories and activities.

Twenty-two years later, the directors and advisors of the Association for Living Values Education International (ALIVE) wish to offer their deep appreciation to the numerous organizations and individuals who have contributed to the development of LVE, and who have implemented LVE in countries around the world. Many dedicated LVE coordinators, trainers, artists and even film makers around the world have served as volunteers. The approach, materials, training programs and projects continue to be developed as new requests for special needs populations are received, and as different countries well versed in the LVE methodology create new materials for their context.

In the early stages of development of LVE, the Brahma Kumaris contributed extensively. They helped edit the initial pilot materials and disseminated LVE through their global network of centers and their relationships with educators. A peace organization deeply interested in values, the Brahma Kumaris continue to provide support or partnership when such is desired by a national LVE group.

Other organizations which also supported LVE in its beginning stages were the Educational Cluster of UNICEF (New York), UNESCO, the Planet Society, the Spanish Committee of UNICEF, the Mauritius Institute of Education and the regional UNESCO Office in Lebanon.

An Independent Organization

In 2004, LVE created its own independent non-profit organization, the Association of Living Values Education International (ALIVE). ALIVE was formed with the aim to benefit more educators, children, young adults and communities through the involvement of a host of other organizations, agencies, governmental bodies, foundations, community groups and individuals. LVE educators in some countries formed their own non-profit LVE associations in order to become an ALIVE Associate while other NGOs became ALIVE Associates. ALIVE Associates and Focal Points for LVE act as the lead for LVE in their country and train educators in schools and agencies to implement LVE. Examples of NGOs who became ALIVE Associates are: Club Avenir des Enfants de Guinée in Guinea Conakry, Yayasan Karuna Bali in Indonesia, Hand in Hand in the Maldives, and the National Children's Council in the Seychelles.

None of the above cooperation would have been possible without the dedication, work and love of the educators who believe in Values Education, the LVE national teams around the world, the ALIVE Associates and Focal Points for LVE, the LVE trainers and volunteers, and those who serve on the ALIVE board and International Advisory Committee. We would like to thank each one of you for your work towards safe, healthy, caring, quality learning environments for children and a better world for all.

Results — Reports, Evaluations and Research

Educator evaluations collected from teachers implementing LVE in countries around the world frequently note positive changes in teacher-student relationships and in student-student relationships both inside and outside the classroom. Educators note an increase in respect, caring, cooperation, motivation, concentration, and the ability to solve peer conflicts on the part of the students. Within a matter of months, educators note that students spontaneously begin to discuss challenges in the language of values, become aware of the effects of values on the self, others and the community, and strive to live their values by making positive socially-conscious choices. Bullying and violence decline as positive social and emotional skills increase. Research also notes academic gains. LVE helps educators co-create with students safe, caring, values-based atmospheres for quality learning.

A Few Observations and Stories

From Kenya: Catherine Kanyi noted, "With LVE the children changed so quickly you could notice which value worked well. Parents also notice the difference in schools implementing LVE. There is no fighting at school. The teacher-pupil relationship is good; there is polite language at school. The parent-teacher relationship is good. Children miss being at school all the time for there is love, peace, freedom and unity."

From Malaysia: Shahida Abdul-Samad, the Focal Point for LVE in Malaysia, wrote about an educator's reaction to an LVE workshop she and Diane Tillman facilitated in 2002. Shahida wrote: "I remember vividly Rahimah's comments after the LVE training ended. She said, 'Shahida, I promise you I will try and implement what I have learnt from you and Diane and see if it works. I will do that. If I see results, I will let you know. That's my commitment to you.'

Every school Rahimah Sura headed she implemented LVE school wide. From inner city schools with major disciplinary problems, to rural schools with drug addiction problems, to the best boarding schools with teachers challenging her positive teaching strategies, she was able in every instance to turnaround each and every school to become the best schools in Malaysia attaining national awards. Children who were drug abusers became actively involved in drama and dance and won competitions locally and nationwide. Teenagers who used to destroy toilets and common facilities changed over a new leaf and took responsibility for the cleanliness of their toilets. They took pride in what they did. Destruction and vandalism dwindled down to zero.

Today these schools are the Exemplary schools. They are rated highest amongst school rankings. From being in the worst band, they moved to the highest band, i.e., from D to A. Not only did this positive environment impact the school and its inhabitants, the positive energy overflowed to their homes and communities, bringing parents, community leaders together — all lending their support to further Rahimah's effort in the 'magic' she created. It wasn't easy for her in the beginning. As usual there was resistance to change. She persisted in the belief that this was the way forward — to bring about change using LVE's Theoretical Model as her compass.

The use of canes was thrown out; students were given the freedom to move from classroom to classroom without being monitored; teachers who refused to follow the LVE approach were counseled and encouraged to use the techniques and activities from the LVE activity books.

With Rahimah's skill set and experience in implementing LVE through PBB, values activities and setting clear guidelines that everyone adhered to, the teachers' hearts and minds began to change. Rahimah once again proved that LVE wasn't just magic or something that happened by chance, it was actually a systematic and well-designed program that brings out the best that is in all of us — our innate values. Rahimah went on to be honored and recognized by the Ministry of Education and was awarded the highest award a civil servant can achieve due to her untiring efforts to bring about positive change through LVE."

From Egypt: A teacher in El-Menia explained that one day she had to leave her class of primary level children unattended for some time. As she was walking back to the class she expected to hear a lot of noise, but to her surprise there was no sound coming from the class. When she reached the class, she found that one of the students was standing and conducting an LVE guided relaxation/ focusing exercise for the rest of the class while all the other students were quiet and calm and enjoying the experience!

Another teacher reported that a girl in her class who used to have the highest record of absences in previous years, recorded the highest rate of attendance after using LVE

♦ Universal values teach respect and dignity for each and every person. Learning to enjoy those values promotes wellbeing for individuals and the larger society.

♦ Each student does care about values and has the capacity to positively create and learn when provided with opportunities.

♦ Students thrive in a values-based atmosphere in a positive, safe environment of mutual respect and care — where students are regarded as capable of learning to make socially conscious choices.

Teaching Values

How do we "teach" values? How do we encourage children and young people to explore and develop values and the complementary social skills and attitudes that empower them to reach their potential? We would all like our children and students to be happy, peaceful, caring, respectful and honest. How can we let them know they can make a difference in this world and help them feel empowered to create and contribute?

Students need many different skills, at all levels, if they are to be able to love values, commit to them, and have the social skills, cognitive discernment and understanding to carry those values with them into their life. It is with this intention that the LVE Theoretical Model and the Living Values Education Activities were constructed. LVE provides methods and activities for educators to actively engage and allow students the opportunity to explore and experience universal values. Students benefit by developing skills to cognitively explore, understand and apply values. After a few weeks, dedicated educators implementing Living Values Education with children ages three to seven find school cultures are infused with more respect, caring, kindness and happiness. Often even children with very negative behaviors change dramatically.

In an effort to understand why this approach works, some educators have asked to know more about LVE's theoretical basis. What methods are used within LVE? The schematic below describes the values exploration and development process utilized. There are two complementary processes. The first is the creation of a values-based atmosphere, the second is the process within the facilitation of the Living Values Education Activities.

Developing Values Schematic — the LVE Method

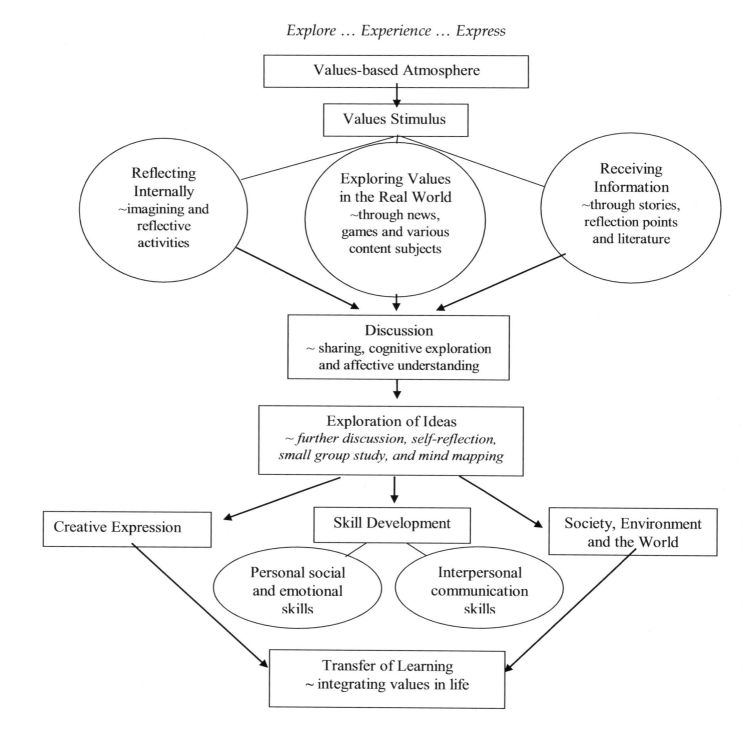

Explore … Experience … Express

Values-based Atmosphere

Values Stimulus

Reflecting Internally
~imagining and reflective activities

Exploring Values in the Real World
~through news, games and various content subjects

Receiving Information
~through stories, reflection points and literature

Discussion
~ sharing, cognitive exploration and affective understanding

Exploration of Ideas
~ *further discussion, self-reflection, small group study, and mind mapping*

Creative Expression

Skill Development

Society, Environment and the World

Personal social and emotional skills

Interpersonal communication skills

Transfer of Learning
~ integrating values in life

Values-based Atmosphere
Feeling Loved, Valued, Respected, Understood and Safe

The establishment of a values-based atmosphere is essential for optimal exploration and development. Such a student-centered environment naturally enhances learning, as relationships based on trust, caring, and respect have a positive effect on motivation, creativity, and affective and cognitive development.

Creating a "values-based atmosphere" is the first step in LVE's Developing Values Schematic. During LVE Educator Workshops, educators are asked to discuss quality teaching methods that allow students to feel loved, respected, valued, understood and safe.

LVE Theoretical Model

The LVE Theoretical Model postulates that students move toward their potential in nurturing, caring, creative learning environments. When motivation and control are attempted through fear, shame and punishment, young people feel more inadequate, fearful, hurt, shamed and unsafe. In addition, evidence suggests that repeated interactions loaded with these emotions marginalize children, decreasing their interest in attending school and/or learning. Students with a series of negative school relationships are likely to "turn off"; some withdraw or become depressed while others enter a cycle of blame, anger, revenge — and possible violence.

Why were these five feelings — loved, valued, respected, understood and safe — chosen for the LVE Theoretical Model? Love is rarely spoken about in educational seminars. Yet, isn't it love and respect that we all want as human beings? Who doesn't want to be valued, understood and safe? Many studies on resiliency have reinforced the importance of the quality of relationships between young people and significant adults in their lives, often teachers.

What happens to the learning process when we feel loved, valued and respected? What happens in our relationships with educators who create a supportive, safe environment in the classroom? Many people have had the experience as a child of an educator who they found positive, encouraging and motivating. In contrast, how do we feel when an educator, at school or home, is critical, punitive and stressed or when the peers are derogatory or bully? While an interesting stimulus can heighten the creative process, high anxiety, criticism, pressure and punitive methods slow down the learning process. Simply the thought that others may be critical or have dislike can distract one from a task. Neurophysiologists have found positive effects on brain development when

Step Two:

Engage yourself and your entire faculty/all the adults in your learning community in an LVE Educator/Facilitator Workshop, to explore the kind of values-based atmosphere you would like to create, learn about skills to do such, and think about how you can make values an important, integral part of your school culture and curriculum. Plan to engage in an ongoing dialogue about values, as you make your organization one which thinks about values when making decisions about, for and with, students and teachers.

Step Three:

Find time to integrate LVE activities. Living Values Education Activities for children ages three to seven are short; 20 minutes is usually sufficient. The activities can be easily incorporated into opening time, circle time, or language arts. Values are naturally reinforced during the entire day when the whole school chooses to focus on one value and the educators are committed to a values-based atmosphere.

Implementation Details

LVE's sixteen values units are designed to allow you to easily plan values education at your site by focusing on one value a month during the school year. Book 1 includes eight values units for the first year of implementation and Book 2 includes another eight values units for implementation during the second year. A "value of focus" each month for the entire school facilitates planning for assemblies and special projects.

The universal values explored are peace, respect, love and caring, tolerance, honesty, happiness, responsibility, simplicity and caring for the Earth and Her Oceans, cooperation, humility, compassion, brave and gentle, and unity. The "Brave and Gentle" values unit substitutes for freedom in the Living Values Education Activities books for older children. Another unit is titled "Another Value We Love". This offers activities on a few values and an invitation to educators to explore a value they feel is needed locally or nationally.

It is recommended that educators begin with the Peace I and Respect I values units in Book 1 during the first year of implementation and Peace II and Respect II values units in Book 2 during the second year. The Quietly Being exercises and conflict resolution skills developed during the Peace I and Respect I values units are important building blocks in creating both a values-based atmosphere and positive social skills.

This book contains at least three values activities for each week. Young people also benefit by songs and the Quietly Being exercise several times a week, or daily.

If a school is planning to begin values education with *only* two grades in a school, it is recommended that you start with the older students/higher grade levels. It is much healthier for younger students to "catch" values from older students who are benefiting from values education, than to have younger students who are into values education being bullied by older students who are not in the program. However, school-wide implementation is more effective and beneficial for all.

Please begin with the Peace Unit!

Beginning with the Peace Unit is always recommended. Young people are often concerned about peace — even at such a young age. At the beginning of the unit, facilitators are asked to engage them in imagining a peaceful world. This allows children to look inside themselves and explore what they would like their world to be like. After a visualization, they are asked to express their ideas verbally and artistically. The opportunity to explore what they would like in the world creates interest and happiness.

Children are then engaged in activities with stories and the making and playing with peace puppets. Lessons with quietly being exercises and art allow them a chance to explore peace at a personal level before conflict resolution activities are begun. Discussions in those lessons help build understanding of others and allow them to further their communication skills.

How many Living Values Education Activities would you suggest I do weekly?

Our internal research shows that educators working with three- to seven-year olds have excellent results when they do three Living Values Education Activities a week and do most or all of the lessons within the values units. It is easier for the children to carry new positive behaviors to the playground when other classes are also implementing LVE. As you integrate the activities into your curriculum, bring values and what the children are learning and discussing into story discussions, social interactions and playground activities. Soon they will be using the language of values to discuss things, and solve many of their challenges independently.

Wonderful practices daily . . .

Sing. Begin or end with a song, as you prefer. Sing songs on the theme of the value with the children, but include the Peace, Respect and Love songs occasionally.

Quietly Being Exercises. Do a Quietly Being exercise once a day. Initially you may wish to alternate daily between the *Peace Star* exercise and the *Respect Star* exercise. After the class has completed the Love unit, do the *Filling Up With Love* exercise every third lesson. For your convenience, these exercises are also in the Appendix. As the values lessons proceed, other exercises are introduced — and perhaps the children would like to make up some of their own.

Circle Time. Providing Circle Time or sharing time daily, or if not possible, once or twice a week, is a wonderful support in creating a values-based atmosphere. It is also a great beginning for values time. The children can sit in a circle if there are less than 15, or if more, they can be grouped in front of the teacher. Ask what they feel good about today, or what they are proud of. Ask them to tell how they showed love or peace to someone, or how they lived the value of focus. Positively acknowledge whatever they share. It is also a good time for children to share any concerns and to engage in group problem solving.

Adapt the Level of Language to Different Ages

Educators will need to adapt the level of language, directions, and the amount of adult assistance to the age of the children. This is especially important for this age range, as language and directions for a three-year old are simpler and more concrete than for a seven-year old. Some of the activities can be adapted for two-year olds.

Assemblies and Songs

If the entire school is exploring the same value for a period of time, a short assembly is often an excellent way to begin or end a values unit. A few teachers could create the first program. After that, different classes of children could take turns doing a song and a skit. Or, the Principal may wish to tell a story and involve a few children from the audience.

Is there a recommended order of values units?

We suggest following the Peace Unit with the values units on respect, love and tolerance/acceptance. The lessons found in the units on peace and respect contain valuable intrapersonal and interpersonal social skills. The quietly being exercises and conflict resolution skills developed during these lessons are important building blocks in creating a values-based atmosphere. If students are able to solve their own conflicts, peacefully and respectfully, there is much more time for teaching.

Do I need to do every activity?

No. While it is good to include a variety of values activities, educators may choose not to do some lessons or may wish to substitute material. In many of the lessons

By now, almost all the Star children had arrived on Earth, and they were joined by many, many Earth children. "We want to be like the Stars," said the Earth children. Suddenly they saw something very bright shining in the sky. It was the Brightest Star together with the Happy Star and the Ever-laughing Star. The Brightest Star beamed at the children, and the Laughing Star had such a funny laugh that the children simply couldn't help but laugh as well.

"Let's have a good time!" sang the Happy Star, and they started to play and sing. The Stars brought yummy treats. It was the best party anyone could imagine. Everyone was happy. They danced, played, ate and laughed. "This is the best party ever!" they agreed.

Then it happened! Nobody had noticed the arrival of the Quiet Star, but then she spoke: "The great Sun Star has sent me to you," she said softly and sweetly. "It's time to go home now."

The children on earth had also been thinking about going home, for it was almost dark. They hugged the stars good-bye.

One of the Peace Stars said softly to the children, "Know that we are always here for you — even in the daytime when you can't see us. Just picture us in your mind, and you will feel our beams of love and peace."

Then the Star children beamed brightly at the children and flew back to the great Sun Star. It was a lovely sight. As the Peace Stars flew higher and higher, they sent bright beams and loving thoughts to the children below.

All the Peace Stars sent peace, and each Peace Star sent his or her own special quality as well. The Patient Star sent patience. The Laughing Star sent a happy laugh. The Quiet Star sent soft, quiet beams. And, the Loving Star sent lots and lots of loving thoughts. The children on Earth watched happily and waved to the stars, "Come back soon," they cried, and then returned home.

Do you think that the children and the Peace Stars ever met again? Do you think that we can become as peaceful, happy, and loving as the Star children?

When finished reading, say: "For a few moments, let's become like the Peace Stars. . . . Relax your body and sit quietly . . . Sit so quietly that you the little star can shine brightly. . . . Each one of you is a beautiful star. . . . When you shine with silence and peace, you bring love into the room. . . ."

Discuss/Share

"The Star Story" and the following Peace Point:

♦ One of the meanings of peace is having good feelings inside.

Ask:

- What were some of the names of the Peace Stars?
- Why did the Peace Stars come down?
- What did the Courageous Star say was the most courageous thing to do? (Not to fight or quarrel.)
- What do all the Peace Stars do when the children picture them?

Activity

Invite the children to color or draw a picture about "The Star Story". The six- and seven-year olds could add a couple of sentences about their picture.

Close with singing the same peace song you sang in the first peace lesson.

PEACE I LESSON 3
Being a Peace Star

Peace Tent Preparation: You may wish to set up a Peace Tent in your room or a special Peace Place. A Peace Tent can be made simply with see-through material hung in one corner of the room, and fastened to the walls to create an opening. The children can sit there when they want to be peaceful.

Begin with a peace song.

Share the Reflection Point:

♦ Peace is feeling quiet inside.

Ask, positively acknowledging all answers:

- Can someone tell me what that means?

Introduction to the Peace Star Quietly Being Exercise: Say, "One way to be peaceful is to be quiet inside. Today, let's practice feeling peaceful. One of the ways we can feel peace inside is to think of the stars and imagine ourselves to be just like them. They are so beautiful in the sky, and they sparkle and shine. They can be seen, but we cannot hear them. They are so quiet and peaceful. I want everyone to be very still . . ."

> ## NOTE TO EDUCATOR
>
> If you feel the children may have difficulty settling down to the following Quietly Being Exercise, lead them around the room first, inviting them to follow you in a line and imitate you as you make peaceful movements with your arms. Play some music and enjoy moving peacefully together.
>
> Many children love to lay on the floor when they do the quietly being exercises. If you wish to try this, ask them to make a circle. Everyone could lay down with their feet toward the middle of the circle. At other times, do the Quietly Being Exercises sitting. It may take them a few times before they settle in easily, but the more you do it, the more they will enjoy "quietly being".

Peace Star Quietly Being Exercise

"For a few moments, think of the stars and imagine yourselves to be like them . . . quiet and peaceful. . . . Let the body be still. . . . Relax your toes and legs . . . relax your stomach . . . and your shoulders. . . . Relax your arms . . . and your face. . . . You are a peace star. . . . What color of peace do you shine with today? . . . Perhaps with a rose color that has a feeling of being safe and loved . . . perhaps a blue color that shines a light of kindness and courage. . . . Or perhaps are like a yellow peace star that shines with the light of peace and happiness. . . . We are peace stars . . . still . . . full . . . relaxed and peaceful. . . . Whenever you want to feel peaceful inside, you can become very still and quiet inside and remember that you are a peace star. . . . Slowly take a big breath in . . . and now slowly breathe out. . . . Wiggle your toes . . and now look around and let yourself shine silently with peace for just a moment."

Note to Educator: The Peace Star Quietly Being Exercise is also in the Appendix.

Activity

Ask each child to make a star. If they are toddlers, you may wish to cut out the stars beforehand. Or, the six-year olds can help the younger children cut them out. Print the first name of each child inside the star. (If this is a new class, you can use these as name tags for the next few days.) Ask the children to decorate the stars with the materials available.

Some educators supply little sticks so that the children can put their star at the top of the stick and wave them very slowly when the educator gives a quiet signal with his or her peace star — or wave them when they sing a peace song.

End with a peace song.

NOTE TO EDUCATOR

Putting Peace into Practice: When you want the children to pause quietly for a few moments, tell them, "For a minute, let's be as peaceful and full of quiet happiness as the stars. . . ." This can be done several times during the day if you like. Wait until they are all quiet — and a few moments longer so they can become peaceful — then affirm their good efforts, saying quietly, "You <u>are</u> peace stars."

Sometimes three- and four-year olds like to hug the Peace Star during the day. They can hug the one made as an example just before the teacher read "The Star Story," or a Star Pillow can be made.

PEACE I LESSON 4

Peace Puppets

Begin with a peace song.

Imagining Peaceful Children in a Peaceful World

Lead the children in this imagining exercise. Say the following, pausing at the dots:

"Today, you can use your imagination to make a picture of a peaceful world in your mind. Let your body be comfortable and very still. . . . Imagine a pretty garden, with trees, and flowers. . . . It's very nice in the garden, the grass is soft, and you can hear birds singing. . . . Imagine the birds flying slowly across the sky. . . . There is a safe and peaceful feeling here. . . . There is a little pond nearby with golden fish swimming slowly. . . . As you walk by the pond, you see a couple of children your age walking toward you. They wave and say hello. . . . The children invite you to play. . . . You picture yourself playing with them. What game do you play?. . . You play for a while and talk for a while. . . . You see other children playing a game nearby, and everyone is happy. Everyone knows how to be kind in this place . . . You continue to have a good time with your friends. . . . And when it is time to go, you all say goodbye. . . . Now bring your attention back here to our classroom."

Discuss/Share

- What was the peaceful world like that you imagined?
- How did the children act?

Sing a peace song together or the following song.

Song: Monster

Chorus: ᴬI don't want to be a monster.

I want peace today.

I don't want to be a monster.

Monster go away!

Verse: ᴬWhen the monster comes out,

ᴮ ᵐⁱⁿI scream and shout.

ᴰHow can I make it go a-ᴬway?

If I cool off awhile,

And ᴮ ᵐⁱⁿput on a smile,

ᴰSoon everything will be o-ᴬkay.

The monster in me

Is ᴮ ᵐⁱⁿalways angry,

ᴰIt wants to fight and never ᴬcares.

So I give myself a hug.

ᴮ ᵐⁱⁿOut comes the love.

And the monster disap-ᴬpears.

(Repeat chorus two times.)

— Contributed by Max and Marcia Nass

Close with the Quietly Being Peace Exercise.

PEACE I LESSON 11
Kindness and Feelings

Begin with a song.

Discuss/Share

Discuss the following Peace Point:

◆ Peace is having good feelings inside.

Ask:

• How do you feel when another child calls you names?

• How do you feel when another child says something nice to you?

- What do you feel when someone does something kind?
- What kind things do you like others to do?
- What kind things do you like to do?
- Do you think your peace puppets have any more ideas about being kind?

Activity

Demonstrate Conflict Resolution: Ask two students to volunteer to enact a pretend problem-solving demonstration.

Ask the children to work in groups of two. Ask each pair of children to draw one picture about the kind things the children like to do and like others to do.

Close with the Peace Star Quietly Being Exercise.

PEACE I LESSON 12
Make Peace Bubbles

Begin with a peace song.

Activity

Part 1. Make a bowl of soapy water and give each child a "bubble maker" to blow bubbles. One by one, each child will blow Peace Bubbles with a Peaceful wish inside. Watch the bubble rise and the pop!

As each bubble pops — ask the child to have a Peaceful Wish — maybe for themselves, others, animals, birds or nature.

When all the children have blown their bubbles, ask them to share their Peace wishes.

Close with more bubble blowing as a group, and then with the Quietly Being Peace Exercise.

Part 2. Create a picture of a tree at the children's height with plenty of branches and draw Peace Bubbles. Add their wish to each bubble and invite other children and parents to view the Peace Bubbles.

Or, if your school has a tree outdoors, add the peace bubbles to the tree and invite parents and friends to view the children's Peace Bubbles.

— Contributed by Dina Eidan and Peter Williams

PEACE I LESSON 13
Conflict Resolution Practice and Posters

Begin with a peace song.

Lesson Content

Step 1. Review the sentence to use when a child is stopping a conflict with another child who is pushing, pinching or shoving:

- ❖ I don't like it when you do that, I want you to stop. Arms are for helping, not for hurting.

Step 2. Review the three things we talk about if there is a conflict:

- ❖ How do you feel?
- ❖ What would you like the other person not to do?
- ❖ What would you like the other person to do?

Step 3. Discuss all three questions with the students as was done in Lesson 10. (Please refer to Lesson 10.) But, this time make a list of all their answers.

Step 4. Demonstrate the Conflict Resolution process a couple of times with children volunteers with a conflict made up about one of the things they mentioned.

Activity

For little children, ask them to draw a picture about the things they want other people to do instead of fight.

For six- and seven-year olds, ask them to form small groups. Each small group can make a picture or poster of things the children want other people to do and do not.

End with the Peace Star Quietly Being Exercise.

NOTE TO EDUCATOR

Putting children in charge of the Conflict Resolution process: Please take time during the next week or two to use this process during the day when the children have conflicts. Then create a solving space for the children to go to when there is a conflict, where the three questions can be posted on the wall with symbols. It could be at a little table, by a little rug on the floor or in the peace tent. Choose one or two children who know the three questions and can listen respectfully, to be conflict resolution mediators. These "Peace Star Helpers" can go to the special solving place to help when others are having a conflict. When all the children have the process down, even the children who used to have more conflicts could serve as Peace Star Helpers.

Share a Story: Lily the Leopard

Lily the Leopard thought there was something gravely wrong with her. Unlike all the other leopards she knew, her spots were not black but pink. It would not have been so terrible if the other leopards had accepted her. But the other leopards would not accept her. In fact, even her own family shunned her. Her mother had cried upon seeing her baby daughter covered in pink spots, and her father and two brothers, Julian and Ricky, were embarrassed to have such a strange looking leopard in the family. The other leopards in the neighborhood ignored her, laughed at her, and even attacked her at times, just because her spots were a different color from their spots. Much of the time she felt afraid and sad, which at times made her very angry. She spent a great deal of time alone.

She spent her days lying in a bush, watching the other leopards frolic about. Even when they would occasionally call Lily to come play, she would remember their past insults and would growl low in response to their invitation.

It was not her fault. She was different and could not help that. She often wondered why the other leopards did not understand. She had done her best to rid herself of her pink spots. Lily tried scrubbing and washing them away. She tried bleaching them. Once, she even painted them black, but the pink soon shone through the paint. It was no good. Nothing worked. After a while, she realized that she was stuck with them. What else could she do?

One day, after four young cubs tried to scratch her, Lily decided to run away from home. She had had enough. She ran off into the jungle as fast as she could. Lily ran for hours and hours, just stopping to rest now and then and to wipe the tears from her eyes.

Eventually she came to rest in a clearing and fell asleep. She was awakened by the soft touch of a tongue on her nose. As she looked up, she saw the most amazing sight. Before her stood a great big leopard with bright green spots!

Lily was so surprised by what she saw that she blinked twice just to make sure she wasn't dreaming. She had often had dreams of other leopards with different colored spots, but she never imagined that there actually were such leopards. The great leopard with bright green spots told her his name was Lenny and asked her what she was doing so far from home. As he spoke, he seemed to glow with confidence and happiness. His eyes were filled with kindness, and so Lily felt safe and soon found herself telling her story.

Lenny quietly listened to her story. When she finished, he gave her a warm hug and helped her dry her eyes. He then smiled at her and said, "What you need is some self-respect."

"I do?" asked Lily. "What's that?"

"Self-respect means liking yourself, even when others do not. It means appreciating all the special things about yourself."

Introduction: Say, "We've been singing about some of the good things that you do. Doing good things helps us respect ourselves. It is also important to know what we were talking about the other day — that each one of us is unique and valuable, and lovable and capable. Filling yourself up with those feelings is what respect feels like inside. Let's have the Respect Star join us Peaceful Stars."

Note to Educator: The Respect Star Quietly Being Exercise can also be found in the Appendix.

Respect Star Quietly Being Exercise

"For a few moments, be very still. . . . Relax your toes and legs . . . relax your stomach . . . and your shoulders. . . . Relax your arms . . . and your face. . . . The Respect Star knows each person brings special qualities to the world . . . You are a beautiful peace star . . . you are lovable and capable . . . you are who you are. . . . You are unique and valuable. . . . Enjoy the feeling of respect inside . . . . Each person has special qualities. . . . Perhaps you are courageous and kind . . . perhaps you are friendly and helpful . . . perhaps you are honest and responsible . . . perhaps you give happiness. . . . You are all stars of peace that are lovable and capable. . . . Let yourself be quiet and peaceful inside. . . . Whenever you want to feel especially good inside, be very still . . . and remember you are a star full of peace, a star full of respect."

RESPECT I LESSON 4

My Hands Song

Creative Activity

Make up a simple song or poem using the words written from the My Hands activity of the previous lesson. Have a good time, making hand movements to go with the words of the song.

The following song was created by children in a nursery in London.

These Little Hands
These little hands, what can they do?
They can paint a picture for Mummy and for you.
These little hands, what can they do?
They can hug you and show I love you.
These little hands, what can they do?

They can play the drums one and two.

These little hands, what can they do?

They can blow a kiss to show I love you.

These little hands, what can they do?

They can gently stroke your cheek and wave hello.

Activity

Invite the children to make a card to show their parents by using the hand prints they made in the last lesson.

Three to Four Activity: Help the children write the following with felt tips on the card: My little hands do good things. They _____. (Write out the child's answer.)

Age Five Activity: Invite the children to write some of the good things their hands do. The children may wish to further decorate their card with shapes of hearts or small drawings.

Close with the Respect Star Quietly Being exercise.

RESPECT I LESSON 5
Each One of Us is Unique

Song: You're Tops

Begin by playing the "You're Tops" a couple of times. It is available for free download on the international LVE site, www.livingvalues.net, under For Schools/Children Ages 3–7/Download Songs.

Moaned the lion, "I can't swing from my tail."

Wailed the hippopotamus, "I can't fly."

Grumbled the giraffe, "I can't hop."

And they all wondered why.

Then the lion shook his head. "I know."

The giraffe nodded. "Me too."

The hippopotamus chuckled bubbles.

The whole zoo knew.

"I can ROAR," said the lion.

"I can reach treetops," said the giraffe.

"I can swim," said the hippopotamus.

"In our own way, we're each tops!"

— Contributed by Madeline C. Nella

Discuss/Share

Ask:

- When the lion moaned, "I can't swing from my tail," what animal do you think he was thinking of that can swing from his or her tail?
- What can the lion do that the monkey can't?
- What can the monkey do that the lion can't?
- When the hippopotamus wailed, "I can't fly," who do you think he was thinking of that can fly?
- When the giraffe grumbled, "I can't hop," what animal do you think she was thinking of that can hop?
- Are all lions the same exact color and are they all the exact same size?
- What about monkeys? Are all their tails the same length?"

Say, "Today's Respect Point is:

♦ Respect is knowing I am unique and valuable.

Share: "Everyone is unique and valuable. No one is exactly the same. We are all different."

Ask:

- What are some of the ways people are different?

Ask the following questions at a quicker pace than usual. The children can raise their hands instead of answering.

- Let's think of what you are good at. Who likes math more than reading?
- Who likes reading more than math?
- Who likes reading and math the same?
- Who loves swimming?
- Who is great at climbing trees?
- What loves to make food in the kitchen?
- Who loves music?
- Who can tap out a rhythm with drums?
- Who can tell what bird is singing by just listening to their song?

want us to take turns around the circle again, but this time I want you to say something good about the person sitting next to you." (indicate right or left)

Close with the Garden of Respect Quietly Being Exercise.

RESPECT I LESSON 11
Conflict Resolution with Respect

Begin with a respect song.

Activity

Note to Educator: This lesson is to reinforce the conflict resolution skills taught is Peace I Lesson 10.

> ➢ Say, "When we have a conflict or misunderstanding with our friends or sisters and brothers, and we have the courage to be willing to talk and understand each other, and we can solve any problem.
>
> Ask:

- Do you remember the three questions that help in understanding and solving the problem?
    - ❖ How do you feel?
    - ❖ What would you like the other person not to do?
    - ❖ What would you like the other person to do?

Say, "Today, we're doing to practice conflict resolution again, but this time I want you to pay special attention to listening with respect, and repeating what the other person said with respect."

Demonstrate the conflict resolution skills with two students, as was done during Lesson 10 of the Peace I Unit. With seven-year olds, ask two more students to come up to be peace monitors, and instruct them to ask the three questions. They can practice asking the questions with respect. Positively acknowledge their successes.

Close with a Quietly Being Exercise of your choice and a peace or respect song.

RESPECT I LESSON 12
A Story from Your Culture

Begin with a song.

Read a story from your culture about valuing or respecting someone or something. Then discuss the story and draw it or enact it.

Close with the Respect Star exercise.

RESPECT I LESSON 13
What I'm Proud Of

Begin with a song.

Discuss the following Respect Point:

♦ Respect is valuing myself.

Ask:

• When do you value yourself?

• When do you feel proud of yourself?

Listen and acknowledge their responses. Tell them each person is valuable, and it is okay to value themselves because they are valuable.

Activity

Ask the children to draw a picture of him or herself doing something each one feels good about or is proud of — or just a picture of the self when he or she is feeling valuable. Allow each child to share if they wish to do so.

Close with a song.

RESPECT I LESSON 14
Crowns

Begin with a song.

Activity

Tell the children that today for the ending activity they can make crowns of their qualities. Provide a piece of paper wide enough to wrap around a child's head. Draw a crown on it with tabs on each end. Draw triangles and diamonds for jewels on another piece of paper. The children can color the crown and the virtue "jewels" and cut them out. The adults can write in the qualities that each child identified if the children are too young to do that for themselves. The jewels can then be pasted on the crown. Help the children make the right size crown by taping or stapling the two end tabs together.

Discuss/Share

With all the children wearing their crowns, ask what they enjoyed during the lessons on respect, and what they learned.

Dance: End with a circle dance while singing "Each One of Us Is Beautiful" or another respect song.

Close with the Respect Star Quietly Being Exercise.

UNIT THREE: LOVE AND CARING

Love and Caring Lessons

The Love and Caring Reflection Points can be used to help define loving and caring behavior and how it works inside. The points can be used as the first focus point during values time, or can be a discussion point as part of language arts. Allow the opportunity to share.

For five- through seven-year olds, the teacher can choose to use some of the words and sentences as content for reading, spelling, and writing.

Love and Caring Reflection Points

- ◆ Love is caring.
- ◆ Love is sharing.
- ◆ Love is being kind.
- ◆ I am good. I am love. All children have love inside.
- ◆ We are always connected to everyone we love.
- ◆ Love means I want what is good for me.
- ◆ Love means I want what is good for others.
- ◆ Safe adults are loving and want what is good for me.
- ◆ Love makes me feel safe.
- ◆ When there's lots of love inside, anger runs away.

Love and Caring Unit Goals and Objectives

Goal: To increase the experience of love.

Objectives:

- ❑ To enjoy the Filling Up with Love Quietly Being Exercise, as demonstrated by sitting quietly during the exercise and appearing content in doing so.
- ❑ To hear and perhaps begin to believe, if they do not: "I am good. I am love. All children have love inside."

❑ To experience feeling love as they listen to "The Invisible String" story.

❑ To enjoy expressing and receiving love nonverbally from their classmates when playing the sponge game.

❑ To paint their feelings of love.

Goal: To increase knowledge about love.
Objectives:

❑ To be able to talk about one or more Love Points.

❑ To hear that feeling sad, grumpy and angry is something that happens to everyone.

❑ To hear, understand and experience that love helps the feelings of sadness, grumpiness and anger go away and to experience being able to fill the self with love.

❑ To finish the root sentence, "I feel full of love when _____."

❑ To participate in a discussion about how love is caring for and helping our friends.

❑ To participate in a discussion about big-hearted people and make suggestions about what mean-hearted people need to know.

❑ To identify loving things people do during values discussions and activities.

Goal: To build sharing and caring social skills.
Objectives:

❑ To make a heart for parents or caregivers.

❑ For ages three to five to make love-filled sponges out of paper and play with them as puppets in a loving space with their classmates.

❑ To hear a song about sharing, to participate in a discussion about sharing and acknowledge that it is hard sometimes, and make a heart-shaped treat for the self and to share with a classmate.

❑ To give their big-hearted creation to someone and tell them why they think they are big-hearted.

❑ To discuss how to do something kind for someone, and to carry out the activity.

❑ To suggest a more appropriate or loving response once the initial negativity in a conflict is identified by others.

Discuss/Share

Ask:

- Where did the sponge live?
- What surprised the sponge when he saw the little girl?
- What did the sponge explain to Marion? When do sponges feel sad?
- What do the sponges do when someone feels sad or angry?
- How were the sponge and Marion the same?

Activity

Three to Five Activity: Instruct the children to make sponges by crumbling up a piece of paper and making two big dots on the outside for eyes. They can then be given five minutes or so to interact with other children, using their love-filled sponge as puppets.

Six and Seven Activity: Invite the children to draw at picture about "The Happy Sponges" story and write one sentence below their picture about the story or their feelings about the story.

Introduce the Filling Up with Love Quietly Being Exercise: Say, "Everyone has love deep inside. But sometimes people forget that it is there, and they don't use it, and so it dries up. And they get sad or angry a lot, because they forgot how to feel all the love that is inside.

- Have you ever been sad? . . . (Wait for their responses and acknowledge.)
- Do you get angry sometimes? . . .

Yes, we all get sad and grumpy and angry sometimes — we forget how we can feel our love inside. So today, we're going to practice feeling the love inside. When we feel lots of love inside, it can grow. This inside love is a special love because it makes us love ourselves and our family and friends even more. Ready to practice?

Filling Up with Love Quietly Being Exercise

"Everyone sit comfortably and let yourself be still inside . . . Let's pretend there is a soft rose-colored circle of light all around us. . . . That rose light is full of love. . . . That love is so soft and light and safe. . . . That light reminds the light inside of me that it's full of love, too. . . . I tune into that rose light inside me and enjoy the fullness of the love. . . . I am me. . . . I am naturally full of love. . . . I tune into the beauty inside myself. . . . This rose light of love is always there. . . . Whenever I want to feel more love inside, I can tune into that factory of love inside and make lots more."

Note to Educator: The above exercise is also in the Appendix.

NOTE TO EDUCATOR
Dealing with a Grumpy Child

If the children are having a grumpy day, you might say, "Do you know what I know when people are grumpy? . . . That there's not enough love inside. Shall we choose love over being grumpy? Okay? . . . But first, does anyone want to share why he or she is grumpy? We're all grumpy sometimes, and that's okay. But, we can do something about it, because it isn't much fun. Who would like to share why he or she is grumpy?" . . .

Acknowledge the responses, and take care of any real physical needs if there are such. For example, if someone is hungry, have snack time first. If someone was fighting, have the children tell how they feel, and resolve the problem using the conflict resolution methods in the Peace unit. Then proceed: "Let's sit down and go to our inside love factory. I let the cloud of grumpiness start to go away as I picture a soft rose-colored circle of light all around us" . . . (Proceed as in the Quietly Being Exercise above).

LOVE LESSON 2
The Sponge Game

Begin by teaching a song on love. Teach one from your culture or you may wish to listen to and sing the course of "The Light of Love" by Michael Turner. On his *Michael Turner and the Peaceful Stars* album, he kindly made it available on the LVE website, livingvalues.net. It can be found under For Schools/Children Ages 3 –7/Songs.

Discuss/Share

The following Love Points:

- ◆ Love is caring.
- ◆ Love is sharing.
- ◆ Love is being kind.
- ◆ Love means I want what is good for others.

Activity

Step 1. Read "The Happy Sponges" story again.

Step 2. Ask the children of ages six and seven to make sponges. They can use real sponges or make them out of crumpled paper. They can decorate them by adding facial features or whatever sparks their imagination. Children ages three through five already made sponges in the last lesson.

Step 3. Ask one-third of the children to form a circle with their sponges, facing outward. As the other children circle around them, they are to hold their sponges up and feel that their sponge is giving love to each child that passes. Play some happy music or have all the children sing as they do this.

Step 4. Give each one-third of the class a turn standing in the middle with their sponges — just two to three minutes or the length of one song. Have a good time.

Close with the Filling Up with Love Quietly Being Exercise

LOVE LESSON 3
Strings of Love

Begin with a song.

Share a Story: The Invisible String

"The Invisible String" by Patrice Karst shares a delightful and reassuring tale of how we are always connected to those we love with an invisible string. The Joy of Reading Project kindly gave their permission to post this story on the international LVE site, www.livingvalues.net. You will find it under For Schools/Children Ages 3–7/Download Free Stories/Love 3–7.

Discuss/Share

Ask:

- What did you like about the story?
- Do you have any questions about the story?
- In the story, could the invisible string of love travel to any person the mother loved?
- In the story, could the invisible string of love travel to any person the children loved?
- When does that string exist? . . . Yes, whenever there is love in your heart.
- Is love stronger than anger? . . . Yes, as long as love is in your heart the string of love will always be there.
- Think for a moment of all the people you care about. . . . (Pause.) Do you have lots of invisible strings? . . . Imagine them. . . . (Pause.) What color might they be?

Say, "One of the Love Reflection Points we can take from the story is:"

- ♦ We are always connected to everyone we love.

Say, "Another Love Reflection Points is:"

- ♦ I am good. I am love. All children have love inside.

Ask, accepting whatever answers they give:

- Did you know that all children are naturally good and loving? Comment: "It's true. All children are naturally good and loving. Each child is born that way. All children have love inside."

Activity Options

String of Love Activity: If you experience a lot of love for the children and they are already at the point of caring and harmony with the other children in the class, play with the string of love idea by interacting with string, yarn, ribbon or long thin strips of paper with the children. Perhaps just play and have fun as you all hold onto the same string in a circle or move/dance in a line or toss the small ball of yarn or string from one to another.

Making Strings of Love Activity: Make strings of love to hang from the ceiling. One way to make them is to use of piece of paper in a circle and then cut a continuous circular pattern closer and closer to the center until it is a long curvy string. Children can imagine what color their string of love would be and pick that color to cut, or color the paper the color they wish. They may wish to decorate it with words or drawings.

Drawings of My Strings of Love for Ages Six and Seven: Children could draw a picture of their strings of love with the people with whom they feel connected and write their feelings about this in sentences below or around the drawing.

Close with the Filling Up with Love Quietly Being Exercise or the Peace Star Quietly Being Exercise.

Homework: If the children's parents have a computer or cell phone at home, perhaps they would like to download "The Invisible String" story from the LVE international site and read it with their children.

LOVE LESSON 4

I Feel Full of Love When . . .

Begin with a song.

Discuss/Share

Ask:

• Do you remember the Love Reflection Points from our last lesson?

♦ We are always connected to everyone we love.
♦ I am good. I am love. All children have love inside.
➢ Say, "Please repeat the last reflection point."

Read "The Invisible String" story, if they would like to hear it again.

In a circle group, ask the children to share the things that make them feel loved or full of love. Positively affirm their ideas.

Root Sentence: Ask the children to stand in a circle and say one sentence beginning with the words, "I feel full of love when _____."

Activity

Provide the opportunity for the children to paint the feeling of love. Ask them to stay in the feeling of being full of love while they paint.

Close with a Quietly Being Exercise.

LOVE LESSON 5
Three Heart Balloons

Educator Preparation: Collect three heart-shaped balloons.

Begin with a song.

Activity: How much love is in your heart?

Step 1. Put or blow air into the three balloons.

For one balloon: Fill it completely with air.

For one balloon: Half fill it with air.

For one balloon: Put in a little air.

Step 2. Ask the children which balloon they prefer. (Most children will say the full balloon.)

Step 3. Share times when you put in full effort with a big heart full of love.

Share times when you are half-hearted and put in a little love.

Share times when you don't really care with little or no love at all.

Step 4. Make a collage of full-hearted balloons full of love.

Step 5. For humor — let the air out of the balloons, one by one.

Reflection: Today, choose to live today with a full heart full of love.

Examples: Talk to someone you usually don't talk to and make a new friend.

Water the plants with love.

Recycle used items with love.

Thank your body for taking care of you.

— Contributed by Eman Arjomand and Peter Williams

LOVE LESSON 6
Hearts and Qualities

Begin with a song.

Ask:

- What kind of world would it be if everyone saw each one's good qualities?
- What kind of world would it be if everyone remembered each one's good qualities all the time?
- What would happen at school?

Activity

Step 1. Give the children materials to make a paper heart. Allow them to color it, or use colored paper. Play relaxing music as they make their hearts.

Step 2. Help those who need it to write their names on the back.

Step 3. Collect the hearts and put them in a box.

Step 4. Take a heart from the box and give one to each child. Each child should receive a heart that is different from his or her own.

Step 5. With five- through seven-year olds, ask them to write a quality of the person whose name is on the heart. For children ages three and four, discuss the qualities of each child and ask them to draw a picture on the heart before giving it back to the other child.

Step 6. Each child can then place the heart in the form of a big heart on the wall with the teacher's help.

— Contributed by Dominique Ache and Encarnación Royo Costa

Homework: Let's practice seeing everyone's good qualities.

LOVE LESSON 7

Love Is Sharing — Heart-Shaped Treats

Share the Love Reflection Point:

- ◆ Love is sharing.

Then play or sing the following song. It can be downloaded free of charge from international LVE site, www. livingvalues.net, under For Schools/Children Ages 3–7/Download Songs.

Song: Share

    Chorus: ^{Db}It's a beautiful feeling to

           Share, share, share

To ^{Gb}show someone you

^{Ab}Care, care, care.

^{Db}You can make friends every ^{Ab}where

When you ^{Ab}learn to ^{Db}share.

Verse: ^{Ab}Will you share your ^{Db}toy with me?

             ^{Ab}And I'll share mine with ^{Db}you.

             ^{Gb}We can ^{Ab}play ^{Db}together

             ^{Eb dim}Instead of one toy ^{Ab}we'll have ^{Db}two!

             ^{Ab}Isn't that Johnny ^{Db}walking by?

             ^{Ab}Let's ask him to ^{Db}play.

             ^{Gb}We'll share ^{Ab}our toys ^{Db}with him

             And ^{Eb dim}make a new ^{Ab}friend ^{Db}today.

(Repeat chorus, repeat verse, and repeat chorus two times.)

— Contributed by Max and Marcia Nass

Read "Piglet Has a Stomach Ache" by Tea Lobjanidze.

Share a Story: Piglet Has a Stomach Ache

Piglet was standing in the yard and eating corn.

"Yummy, yummy! I love corn so much!" piglet said.

"Give me some corn, please! We are friends, are not we?" said the rooster.

"Yes, we are friends. But I have only a little corn. If I had a lot I would offer you some," replied Piglet.

"Give me one grain at least!" said the rooster.

"No, I won't give you any. Even if you are my friend, it doesn't mean I should give you corn, does it? Why should I? I can eat it alone and I will end up having more of it!" answered the piglet and he continued eating the corn.

Soon, Piglet's friend the turkey came by. "Give me some corn! We are friends!" said the turkey.

"Yes, we are friends, but I love corn so much."

"Give me at least one grain!" pleaded the turkey.

"No, I won't give you any. Even if you are my friend, it doesn't mean I should give you corn, does it? Why should I? I can eat it alone and I will end up having more of it!" answered the piglet and he continued eating the corn.

- Think of someone that's loving. What is he or she like?
- What kind of things does that person do?
- Think of loving, safe adults. What do they want for you?
- What do you want for the person you love?

Acknowledge their responses and expand on this theme.

- Does your mother (father, caregiver) want you to eat things that are good for you? Why? (That's right. She or he loves you and wants you to be healthy. She or he wants what is good for you.)
- Does your father (mother, caregiver) want you to smoke? Why not?

Activity

Ask the children to role play as the loving safe person who wants something good for them. They can enact various roles: mother and child, father and child, child and child, etc.

Note to Educator regarding unsafe adults and inappropriate touching: If you are concerned about unsafe teens or adults touching children inappropriately, this is a good time to bring up the topic. One helpful story for children of this age is "My body belongs to me from my head to my toes" by Pro Familia. The Joy of Reading Project kindly gave their permission to make it available on the international LVE site, livingvalues.net. It is under For Schools/Children Ages 3–7/Download Stories/Love 3–7.

Close with a Quietly Being Exercise of your choice.

LOVE LESSON 15

Love Is Being Kind

Begin with a song.

Discuss/Share

The following Love Point:

♦ Love is being kind.

Ask the children to think of ways to show love. Perhaps helping to get things for our moms and dads when they are ill; being helpful and doing extra chores when someone is busy; saying hello to our guests; being friendly to a new child in school; making a card for someone who is ill, a child who is moving, or . . . ?

Activity

Create ideas pertinent to your situation and the ages of the children, and carry out one of those ideas.

LOVE LESSON 16

Celebrating Love and Caring

Discuss/Share

Ask:

- What did you enjoy most during our time on Love and Caring in the last few weeks?
- What did you learn?
- What kind of world would it be if everyone had love for each other?

Activities

Name each child and positively affirm the things he or she did.

Sing some of the songs the children learned during this values unit.

Play the Sponge Game or another activity the children enjoyed.

End with the Filling Up with Love exercise.

UNIT FOUR: TOLERANCE

Tolerance/Appreciation Lessons

The Oxford Dictionary defines tolerance as "The ability or willingness to tolerate the existence of opinions or behavior that one dislikes or disagrees with." The Random House College Dictionary, defines tolerance as "a fair and objective attitude toward those whose opinions, practices, race, religion, nationality, or the like, differ from one's own; freedom from bigotry." This values unit includes this meaning and adds the broader dimension of actively respecting and appreciating other cultures.

Tolerance is used by the United Nations and in political arenas as the name of the value which allows people of different cultures to coexist with mutual understanding, dignity and respect. "The United Nations is committed to strengthening tolerance by fostering mutual understanding among cultures and peoples. This imperative lies at the core of the United Nations Charter, as well as the Universal Declaration of Human Rights, and is more important than ever in this era of rising and violent extremism and widening conflicts that are characterized by a fundamental disregard for human life."

On November 16, 1995, "UNESCO's Member States adopted a Declaration of Principles on Tolerance. Among other things, the Declaration affirms that tolerance is neither indulgence nor indifference. It is respect and appreciation of the rich variety of our world's cultures, our forms of expression and ways of being human. Tolerance recognizes the universal human rights and fundamental freedoms of others. People are naturally diverse; only tolerance can ensure the survival of mixed communities in every region of the globe." (Source: United Nations website)

Some educators have shared that students relate more easily to the word appreciation. This is especially true for young children.

If children are raised by parents who are not prejudiced, they relate beautifully to children of all races, religions and cultures. Educators are immensely important in contributing to the fabric of social cohesion in society by modeling acceptance and appreciation of all.

Very young children usually assume that everyone is like them and are generally not aware of many aspects of their life being part of their culture. Hence, this unit will start with activities to build knowledge and appreciation of their own culture.

While in this unit on tolerance the appreciation of others' cultures is the primary focus, a couple of lessons also take up another meaning: the ability to endure a hardship, or something unpleasant or difficult.

Continue to play a song daily if you and the students are enjoying this. When studying different cultures, perhaps bring in some of that culture's songs and music at the beginning of the lesson. Perhaps sing or listen to songs that speak of the world's peoples as family. For example, "One Family" by Red Grammer speaks of the human world family as "sisters and brothers, a coat of many colors."

Do one of the Relaxation/Focusing exercises every day or every several days, as suitable for your class.

Tolerance/Appreciation Reflection Points

- ◆ We are all unique and have something valuable to offer and share.
- ◆ Tolerance is appreciating differences.
- ◆ Appreciating our differences grows peace.
- ◆ Tolerance is being open to everyone's beauty.
- ◆ Tolerance is respecting each other's culture.
- ◆ Tolerance grows with respect and understanding.
- ◆ Love for all others grows tolerance.
- ◆ We are all part of one human family.
- ◆ We know how to appreciate the good in others.
- ◆ Tolerance is the ability to stay light.
- ◆ Tolerance is accepting myself, even when I make mistakes.
- ◆ Tolerance is accepting others, even when they make mistakes.

Tolerance/Appreciation Unit Goals and Objectives

Goal: To build a feeling of comfort, belonging or inclusion with the understanding that all people are part of one human family.

Objectives:

❑ To hear from the teacher that we are all part of one human family.

❑ To have the feeling that any child could be their friend by singing the song "Friends Make the World Go Round".

❑ To hear from the teacher that all races and cultures are important for the beauty of the human rainbow.

❑ To reflect on and finish the root sentence, "Human being are one family because _____," and hear the all of their classmates' responses.

Goal: To increase appreciation for their own culture and different cultures.
Objectives:

❑ To learn about the majority culture in the local area through being part of a discussion on the language and race of that culture as well as discussing the common greetings, food and music, etc.

❑ To participate in an activity of the majority culture, be it making a craft, dancing a traditional dance, hearing stories or eating some of the favorite foods.

❑ To learn about a minority culture or two through being part of a discussion on the language and race of that culture as well as discussing the common greetings, food and music, etc.

❑ To participate in an activity of a minority culture or two, be it making a craft, dancing a traditional dance, hearing stories or eating some of the favorite foods.

❑ To be happy about their own culture by bringing a cultural item from home and sharing it with the class.

❑ To understand through the "Josh the Dragon" story that it is okay to not be the same as everyone else; it is okay to be unique — or "different".

❑ To understand that all races and cultures are important for the beauty of the human rainbow.

❑ To hear stories from three different cultures.

Goal: To increase tolerance through compassion.
Objectives:

❑ To understand that people often feel sad when others are mean to them or exclude them because they are different.

Goal: To build tolerance/acceptance/patience with the self.
Objectives:

❑ To not be frustrated when making a small mistake on classwork.

❑ For children with sufficient language ability to state the rule, "It's okay to make a mistake; all I have to do is correct it."

TOLERANCE LESSON 1

Learning About the Majority Culture

Note to Educator: In some countries, and in certain areas of other countries, there is one culture, one race and one religion. In other countries, there are many races and cultures. In a monocultural society, very young children assume that everyone is like them and are not aware of many aspects of their life being part of their culture. Hence, it is important to build knowledge and appreciation of their own culture before venturing into building knowledge and appreciation of other cultures. For educators who are in multicultural societies, please start with the culture of the majority of children in your class/school.

Educator Preparation: Please plan to do a traditional or folk dance with the children from their culture, using music from their culture.

Begin with a song about love, togetherness or being one world family.

Discuss/Share

Introduce: "In the next few weeks we are going to learn about tolerance. Adults sometimes use the word tolerance to mean appreciating everyone's culture and race."
Ask:

- What does appreciating mean? Great. Give me an example.

Tolerance/Appreciation Point:

- ♦ Tolerance is respecting each other's culture.
- ♦ Love for all others grows tolerance.

Say, "Let's start understanding tolerance by looking at our culture (or, the culture of most of the people in this room)."
Ask:

- Today we will talk about the _____ culture. What is the language of the _____ culture?
- What language do your parents speak?
- What language do your grandparents speak?
- What is the traditional dress in the _____ culture? (Discuss and go into depth in this area, in an age appropriate way. Is there a traditional dress that is only worn on certain occasions?)

- What are some of the traditional festivals or holidays? (Discuss and go into depth in this area, in an age appropriate way.)
- How do you greet your elders?
- What is the race of the people of the _____ culture called?
- What are some of the favorite foods in the _____ culture?
- What artistic things are created in the _____ culture?
- What else do you like about the _____ culture?
- What are the traditional musical instruments in the _____ culture?

Activity

Begin to play some of the music from the culture of the children, and invite them to dance. They may need to be taught a traditional or folk dance.

Homework: Ask the children of the _____ culture to bring something from home that is traditional in that culture. This might be a picture of their parent in the traditional dress, a traditional piece of clothing, a food item, an ornament, a musical instrument, etc. If you are not in a monocultural setting, tell the children that they will all have the chance to bring in something from their home when you are studying their culture.

Close with a Quietly Being Exercise.

TOLERANCE LESSON 2

Something that I Like About My Culture

Begin with a song from the _____ culture which you focused on during the last lesson.

Activities

Show and Tell Activity: Invite each of the children from the _____ culture to show the item they brought from home to the entire group and tell about it.

Dance/Musical Activity: After they share, play the music you played at the last lesson and involved all the children in dancing the traditional dance.

Close with a Quietly Being Exercise.

TOLERANCE LESSON 3

Sharing Something from the Majority Culture

Educator Preparation: If you are in a monocultural setting, plan to tell the children a little about their history, or invite special people from the community that can tell some of the traditional stories/tales, or demonstrate a special craft for which the culture is known.

If you are in a multicultural setting, it would be inclusive to involve all the children in learning a traditional craft, creating something artistic in the style or with the method of that culture, or making a special treat to eat from the majority culture. Perhaps a couple of the parents would like to help with this.

Begin with a song about love, togetherness or being one world family or a traditional song from the _____ culture.

Activity: Carry out the activity you planned after reading the Educator Preparation note above.

Close with the Garden of Respect Quietly Being Exercise.

TOLERANCE LESSON 4
All Kinds of Friends

Song: Friends Make the World Go Round

Begin by playing the following song. It can be downloaded free on the international LVE website, livingvalues.net under For Schools/Children Ages 3–7/Download Songs.

Chorus: BbFriends Make the EbWorld Go BbRound
EbFriends Make the EbWorld Go BbRound
Friends Make the EbWorld Go BbRound
EbFriends Make the World Go BbRound

EbThey'll bring you a Fsmile
When Ebyou've got a Bbfrown
EbGive you a Flaugh
When Ebyou're feeling Bbdown
CmFriends come in Fred, yellow
CmBlack, white and Fbrown
Yes, Bbfriends make the Ebworld go Bbround
EbFriends make the world go Bbround

Verse: BbA new kid moves Am dimin one day.

129

^{Bb}I ask, would you ^{Am dim}like to play?

We ^{Bb}swing on the ^{Am dim}monkey bars.

^{Bb}Make believe we ^{Am dim}touch the ^{Bb}stars.

We talk about ^{Am dim}things we like.

^{Bb}Flying kites and ^{Am dim}riding bikes.

She ^{Bb}said I'm glad ^{Am dim}I met you.

I ^{Bb}said that I ^{Am dim}was glad ^{Bb}too.

(Repeat chorus.)

Verse: ^{Bb}Eat ice cream and ^{Am dim}play some more,

^{Bb}Roam around like ^{Am dim}dinosaurs.

^{Bb}Make some funny ^{Am dim}faces too,

^{Bb}Acting like we're ^{Am dim}at the ^{Bb}zoo.

But ^{Bb}then we (both) have ^{Am dim}to go home,

^{Bb}So I call her ^{Am dim}on the phone.

Ask ^{Bb}if she can ^{Am dim}play again.

^{Bb}It's so much fun ^{Am dim}making ^{Bb}friends.

(Repeat chorus two times.)

— Contributed by Max and Marcia Nass

Read "Josh the Dragon" by Diana Hsu to the children. If you read that story to the children a couple of years ago, there is an alternative story in the Appendix, Item 2: "Who can I play with?"

Share a Story: Josh the Dragon

Once upon a time, there lived a big dragon. His name was Josh. One day while Josh was sitting under a big green tree, he thought, "Oh, how nice it would be to have a friend to play with." So that sunny morning, Josh went away, far away, to look for another dragon to be his friend. On his way he met Ethan the elephant.

"Hi," said the elephant with twinkling eyes, "my name is Ethan! What's your name?"

"Josh," he said, "and I'm looking for a friend — a dragon friend that is." Josh examined Ethan for a moment and then said rather suspiciously, "You have big ears and a long nose. You are not a dragon, are you?"

"No" said the elephant, "but that does not matter, does it? I can still be your friend. You see, I'm looking for a friend, too. I've been feeling sort of lonely lately."

But Josh was not listening to Ethan. He looked at Ethan with coolness and then turned around and trotted off. Ethan, with great sadness, watched Josh leave.

As Josh moved on, he saw a lion. The lion leapt forward with great eagerness. The lion then shook his brilliant mane and smiled at Josh. "What are you doing?" asked the lion.

Josh watched the lion for a moment. Josh had never seen a lion before and was amazed by his beauty. "Oh" he finally replied, "I'm looking for a friend. My name is Josh."

"Oh, I'm looking for a friend, too. My name is Ali, Ali the lion. Come, let's play together. How about having a race or playing a game of tag?" Ali jumped and twirled in anticipation.

At first Josh felt a rush of happiness, but then he suddenly remembered that Ali wasn't a dragon. Josh looked into Ali's smiling face and said, "But you can't be my friend! You are not a dragon." And before the lion could say anything more, Josh turned and ran away.

As Josh was traveling down a country road, he met a little white rabbit. The little rabbit was a bit shy. It hid behind a huge tree, listening carefully with his big long ears and peeking out behind the tree with only one eye. When the little rabbit saw the dragon he thought, "What a big dragon. I hope it's a friendly dragon, otherwise I will have to run away and hide." As Josh came nearer, the little rabbit whispered, "Excuse me, are you a friendly dragon?"

Josh really was a friendly dragon, so the little rabbit did not have to be afraid. The little rabbit just sat quietly behind the tree and watched Josh. Josh also sat under the same tree where the little rabbit was hiding.

Something very amusing caught Josh's attention just a few trees away. There was a clown laughing with great heartiness as he toppled over his huge shoes. Every time the clown toppled over his feet, he lay on his back and laughed and laughed and laughed. Suddenly, Josh realized that he was laughing too and like the clown, Josh laughed and laughed and laughed. They both laughed until they had the hiccups, and that made them both laugh even harder. Josh finally got up and went over to the clown and said: "Hi there, you are a funny clown! I never ever in my whole dragon life laughed so much!"

"You are not the only one. Go ask the children, and they will tell you that I make children laugh and laugh and help them forget all their troubles! I love to make people happy. What do you like to do?" asked the jolly clown.

"Well, I'll tell you what I'd like to do," replied Josh in great seriousness. "I'd like to

If the children in your class are from one culture, vary the activity by asking them to think of another culture or country they have heard of, perhaps on the television or in a movie. Ask the children to think of something from another culture. If they wish, they can bring something from home – or they can think about another culture in another part of the world. Perhaps they can ask their parent about another country they like.

Close with a Quietly Being Exercise.

TOLERANCE LESSON 9
A Tree of Treasures

Begin with a song.

Discuss the Tolerance Reflection Points:

♦ We are all unique and have something valuable to offer and share.

♦ We know how to appreciate the good in others.

Activity

To accept "the universe" of each other, invite each child to bring from home something he or she likes. Or, depending on the circumstances, ask each child to make a small drawing of one of his or her favorite things — perhaps a toy, an activity, or a food.

Draw a tree on a large sheet of paper and allow the children to put their small drawing on the tree.

Help them learn about other countries by showing them where these countries are on a globe and celebrating how children around the world like many of the same things.

Talk about how each one is unique, and how wonderful the tree is because it has so many different types of treasures.

— Contributed by Encarnación Royo Costa

Close with a Quietly Being Exercise.

TOLERANCE LESSON 10
Dances and Foods from A Variety of Cultures

Begin with a song.

Activity

Look at the variety of cultures the class has studied. Revisit each culture, doing something from each culture, such as a dance, singing a song, or eating a special food.

Perhaps some parents could help.

If there is a small group, ask the children to share something they are proud of about their culture — or something they like about the culture of another. The group could make a television frame out of cardboard, and the children can share from behind the frame. Lead the children in applauding each child.

— Contributed by Dominique Ache

Close with a Quietly Being Exercise.

TOLERANCE LESSON 11
Liking Myself — Even When I Make A Mistake

Begin with a song.

Discuss/Share

Introduction: Talk about tolerance for the self — accepting and liking myself, even when I make a mistake. It is important to have tolerance and patience when mistakes are made.

Tell them a rule: "It's okay if you make a mistake; just try to correct it. We don't need to become angry or sad or to feel bad. Sometimes we do become angry at ourselves, or we feel sad or bad. That's because we don't know the rule: It's okay if you make a mistake; just try to correct it." This is a rule the adults can help the children use throughout the year, especially when the children are experiencing difficulty with a task.

— Contributed by Thomas R. Bingham

Discuss the Tolerance Reflection Points:
- ♦ Tolerance is the ability to stay light.
- ♦ Tolerance is accepting myself, even when I make mistakes.
- ♦ Tolerance is accepting others, even when they make mistakes.

Ask:
- Can you remember a mistake you made in math?
- Did you need to feel bad? (No.)
- Were you able to correct it?
- What are other mistakes have you made?
- Great example. Can you tell me what the correction for that mistake would be?

Generate another few examples, helping them see mistakes as part of the learning process. Mistakes means you are trying and making a correction means you are learning!

- What are other mistakes have you made?

- Great example. Can you tell me what the correction for that mistake would be?

- What if I accidently bumped into you and you fell. What would I do?

❖ Yes, I would say, "Oh, I'm sorry. Are you okay? And if you are still sitting on the floor, I might help you up. Yes?

- What if you accidently step on someone's toe? What would you do? (Yes, saying "I'm sorry. Are you okay?" is important.)

➢ Please teach them any other polite phrases in your culture that are appropriate for different circumstances in which mistakes are made.
  Ask:
  - What if someone accidently bumps into you and then says they are sorry. What would be good to do?
  - What other things do people do accidently that you don't like?
  - Can you forgive them and accept their apology?
  - What thoughts help you do that?

Read a story from the children's culture about something or someone with a tolerant and patient attitude.

Close with a Quietly Being Exercise.

TOLERANCE LESSON 12
Human Beings Are One Family Because . . .

Begin with a song from one of the cultures you have been exploring or sing the Friend song together.

Activity

Step 1. Review the cultures you have studied by asking the children what they liked about the unit on tolerance: the stories they remember, what they learned, and what they liked doing.

Step 2. Read one of the stories they want to hear again.

Step 3. Root Sentence: Ask the children to stand in a circle and finish the sentence, "Human beings are one family because _____."

Step 4. Do one of the cultural dances together.

Close with a Quietly Being Exercise.

UNIT FIVE: HONESTY

Honesty Lessons

Honesty Points help define the value. The points can be used as the first focus point during values time, or can be a discussion point as part of language arts. Allow the children the opportunity to share their experiences about that value.

For five- through seven-year olds, the teacher can choose to use some of the words and sentences as content for reading, spelling, and writing. As the students continue with the unit, they can create their own Honesty Points. They can then draw or write those, or make up short stories.

Honesty Reflection Points

- ◆ Honesty is telling what really happened.
- ◆ Honesty is telling the truth.
- ◆ Honesty is when you don't tell a lie and you don't cheat.
- ◆ Honesty is keeping your promises.
- ◆ When I feel honest, I feel clear inside.
- ◆ When I am honest, I can learn and help others learn to be giving.
- ◆ The heart of honesty is fairness.
- ◆ Honesty creates trust.

Honesty Unit Goals and Objectives

Goal: To increase appreciation of honesty.
Objectives:
- ❑ To become aware of an example of being rewarded for honesty by hearing and/or acting out the story, "The Emperor and the Flower Seed."
- ❑ To talk or draw about feelings when someone breaks a promise.

Goal: To increase understanding about honesty.

Objectives:

- ❏ To talk about one of the Honesty Points, such as honesty means telling the truth or honesty means telling what really happened.

- ❏ To be able to distinguish between telling the truth and not telling the truth when the adult demonstrates by saying what he or she is doing with an object.

- ❏ To participate in a discussion after playing the Croak or Buzz game to explore how cheating would ruin the game.

- ❏ To think about how they would feel if there were half the number of cookies as children in the room and how they would like them distributed; to hear that honesty is being fair and greedy is being unfair.

- ❏ To understand that being sneaky is part of dishonesty after hearing "Jade and the Giant" story.

- ❏ To think about honesty as being true to oneself and to answer the question: What qualities or values make me feel true to myself?

Goal: To build honesty skills.

Objectives:

- ❏ To have fun practicing telling the truth with body movements; for ages five to seven to tell the truth about the movement they just did after they did it.

- ❏ To participate in a discussion about why people sometimes don't tell the truth, the consequences when we don't tell the truth, and how telling the truth takes one minute of courage; to practice telling only the truth for one morning.

- ❏ To play a game in the classroom in which the children find a drawing of someone's favorite toy, report it missing, and return it to the owner.

- ❏ To tell a real story or share something that really happened when interviewed on the pretend television.

HONESTY LESSON 1

A Mirror

Begin with a song.

Discuss/Share

Introduce: "In the next few weeks, we're going to learn about honesty."

saw Mohammed and his mother" versus "One day I was walking down the street, and all of a sudden I saw a big green foot! It was as big as a house!"

Close with a Quietly Being Exercise.

HONESTY LESSON 8
One Minute of Courage

Begin with a song.

Only do this unit if there are children in the group who are having difficulty with honesty <u>and</u> they are five years or older. Be light about this topic, and remember that developmentally most children do not have a firm grasp on the difference between reality and fantasy until they are about four or five years old.

Start by bringing up for discussion why people sometimes do not tell the truth. "We've been talking about honesty."

Ask:

• Why do you think people sometimes don't tell the truth?

Say, "Yes, often it is because they don't want to get in trouble or because they don't want somebody to get mad at them or be disappointed in them. We all want people to love us. It sounds like that is what happens with us sometimes, too. . . . So, we sometimes try to hide what happened so we don't get in trouble and so they don't get mad or disappointed."

Ask:

• But what happens when people find out we lied?

Say, "Yes, that's right. They get even more angry and more disappointed, and we get in even more trouble. And although adults may not look so clever sometimes, usually they can figure out the truth fairly well! And if we lie once, they may not trust us to tell the truth another time."

Ask:

• Do we want people to trust us?

Say, "It's important to tell the truth so that our relationship has trust. When there's lots of truth in the relationship, we feel safe and very loved. But, it sometimes takes courage to tell the truth when, for instance, something goes wrong, or when we did something we weren't supposed to do, or when we didn't do something we were supposed to do. But let's see if we can practice telling the truth all morning."

Check in with the children at lunch and ask them to continue practicing the rest of the day. Positively reinforce their efforts. If a child looks like he or she is not going to tell the truth, use the reminder, "One minute of courage . . ."

Activity

Invite the children to draw a picture or write a story about their own experiences. They could also make up simple poems about honesty. For example:

> I am honest,
> I am true.
> When I'm not,
> I am blue.

Close with a Quietly Being Exercise.

HONESTY LESSON 9
Lost and Found

Begin with the song "Friends Make the World Go Round" or another one of your choice.

Discuss/Share

- How would you feel if you lost your favorite toy?
- How would you feel if someone found your toy and returned it to you?
- How would you feel if you lost your lunch money (or something equivalent)?
- How would you feel if someone saw you drop your money and returned it to you?
- How would you feel if someone stole your favorite toy?

Acknowledge the children's feelings and responses. Acknowledge that it is not nice for someone to do that.

Say, "Some people are not honest. Some people are very greedy. What do greedy people say? They say, 'It's all for me! It's all mine!' And they take what belongs to others."

Activity

Step 1. Say, "Let's have a lost-and-found game today." Instruct each child to make a picture of his or her favorite toy on a colored piece of paper.

Step 2. Play a game in the classroom in which half the children close their eyes while the other half hides their colored piece of paper.

Step 3. The children who had their eyes closed now open their eyes and search the room to find one of the hidden drawings. As each one finds a drawing, he or she is to come up to the teacher and say, "Teacher, look what I found!"

Step 4. The teacher can thank each child and then ask the class whose it is. The "finder" can then hand it to the owner. (Encourage the owner to thank the "finder".)

Step 5. Ask the children if they would rather have someone find their toy and keep it. Enjoy their responses.

Step 6. Invite the other half of the class to do the same game.

Discuss the following Honesty Points:

♦ When I feel honest, I feel clear inside.

♦ When I am honest, I can learn and help others learn to be giving.

♦ The heart of honesty is fairness.

Close with a Quietly Being Exercise.

HONESTY LESSON 10
The Heart of Honesty is Fairness

Begin with a song.

Discuss/Share

♦ The heart of honesty is fairness.

Say, "Let's pretend we have 12 cookies. (Use a number that is half of the number of children in your class.)

Ask:

• If there were a really greedy person in the room, which might he or she want to do with the cookies?

• Would you like the greedy person to do that?

• Would that be fair or unfair?

- What does that mean?
- Can anyone tell me about that?
- Can you think of a time that happened?

In a circle group, ask the children to share the things that make them happy. Ask each child to act it out from his or her chair or in the middle of the circle. Their responses might include a smile, a hug, or a fun game. Acknowledge their responses. Lead the applause.

In a circle group, ask the children to share how they give happiness. Ask them to act it out with the child sitting next to them.

Sing a song on happiness from your culture, or you might want to sing the following song. It is available on the LVE international website, www.livingvalus.net under For Schools/Children Ages 3–7/Download Free Songs.

Song: Happy Children

^DDo you see the happy children,

^{A7}Getting up to dance around,

^DAll they want is to be happy,

And to ^{A7}swing and swing around.

^GBend right down and ^Dtouch your toes,

^{A7}Touch your knees and ^Dtouch your nose,

^GClap your hands and ^Dshake them out,

^{E7}Stand upright and ^{A7}turn around . . .

(Repeat)

HAPPINESS LESSON 2
Using Our Imagination

Begin with a song.

Imaginative Activity

Ask the children to sit comfortably or lie on the floor. Say, "Today we're going to use our imagination again to make a picture in our mind. Let yourself get comfortable and let the body be very still. . . ."

"Imagine a big, beautiful butterfly. It can be any color you like. This butterfly likes to fly to places where only happy people live. Do you want to go there, too? . . . Okay, close your eyes and listen. Imagine you are sitting on the wings of this big, beautiful, colorful butterfly and are flying to a place where children are happy. . . . The butterfly begins to come down. You have arrived. . . . Can you see the happy faces of the children? . . . Now the butterfly comes to rest on the grass in this beautiful world, and all the children come to welcome the butterfly and to welcome you. . . . What do they say to you? . . . The children ask you to play with them . . . What are you playing? . . . Now they call you to join a picnic on the grass. . . . What do you eat? . . . What do you say to each other? . . . Now you look around. . . . You see trees, flowers . . . birds . . . the sun. . . . Is your face looking happy? . . . Now it's time to come back to school (or camp or wherever the setting is). You sit on the wings of your loving butterfly, and off you fly back here. Now open your eyes, and we will share."

Share: Ask the children to share their experiences.

Activity

Three to Four Activity: Tell the children that they get to pretend to be happy butterflies. Perhaps they can go outside and run around and wave their arms as though they are wings, and interact with the other butterflies with happy smiles and words.

Five to Seven Activity: Provide the opportunity for children to make butterflies or a picture of a happy world. Paper wings of a butterfly can be painted or colored and attached to an ice cream stick. The butterflies can be used as a Quietly Being symbol, or used to role play conversations.

Close with a Quietly Being Exercise.

HAPPINESS LESSON 3
Happiness Is Knowing I am Loved

Begin with a song.

Discuss/Share

Say, "When we did the unit on respect, we learned that part of respect is knowing we are lovable and capable. Each one of us is loved. But, let's talk about who loves you.

One of the Happiness Points is:

♦   Happiness is knowing I am loved."
Ask:

- What does that mean?
- Why do you think that's true?
- Who loves you?
- Does everyone need to be loved?
- How do people let others know they love them?
- How do you let people know you love them?
- How do you love yourself?

Activity

Ask the children to draw a picture of themselves with someone who loves them.

Homework: Tell the children that their homework for today is to give someone at home one extra hug.

Follow-up to Hug Homework: When they come back the next day, ask the children to tell what happened with their hug homework. Ask, "Is giving a hug to someone we love one of the ways we can give happiness?" If you get a resounding yes, tell the children that their homework for today again is to give someone at home one extra hug. When they come back the next day, ask them what happened, and give them the same homework every day for that week.

Close with a Quietly Being Exercise.

HAPPINESS LESSON 4

Happy Games

Begin with a song.

Discuss the following Happiness Point:

♦   Happiness is having fun with my friends.

Activity

Play a game that everyone loves which brings lots of laughter. You know the ones they love. Many children enjoy Duck, Duck, Goose. In this game, all the children sit in a circle. One child walks around the outside of the circle and gently taps the other children on the top of the head. Each time the child taps, she or he says, duck or goose. The child may say duck one or ten times, but as soon as she or he says goose, the child tapped gets up to chase the tapping child around the circle. The tapping child tries to run all the way around the circle to sit in the place of the child who was called goose. The tapping child may stay there if she or he reaches there without being tagged. Then the other child continues the game by tapping children and saying, duck, duck, duck . . . goose. If tagged, the child must take a turn tapping again.

An adaptation of the game Hide-and-Seek is fun. One person hides and all the rest look for him or her. When the hiding person is found by one child, instead of that ending the game, that person also hides with the hiding person. The game is over when all the children are hiding together. With small groups of little children, the end of the game is a perfect time for forming a circle, holding hands, and singing a song!

The following song is available on the LVE international website under For Schools/Children Ages 3–7/Download Free Songs.

Song: Smile

Chorus: ᴬThe world needs your ᴱsmile
To ᴰᵇremind ᴬeveryone
That we're ᴰᵇhere to be ᴬhappy
So ᴱ⁷smile and have ᴬfun
The ᴬworld needs your ᴱsmile
ᴰᵇSmile all day ᴬthrough
ᴰᵇAnd watch the ᴬwhole world
ᴱ⁷Smile back at ᴬyou.

Verse: ᴰᵇSmile, ᴬsmile, ᴰᵇsmile at ᴬeveryone
ᴰᵇSmile, ᴬsmile, ᴰᵇsmile and have ᴬfun
ᴰᵇSmile, ᴬsmile, ᴰᵇsmile all day ᴬthrough
ᴰᵇSmile, ᴬsmile, ᴰᵇthe world smiles at ᴬyou.

(Repeat chorus, repeat verse, repeat chorus two times.)

— Contributed by Max and Marcia Nass

HAPPINESS LESSON 5

Words Can Be Like Flowers or Thorns

Begin with a song.

Introduce the topic, "Part of happiness comes with words. You were telling me the other day that . . . (Give some examples of what they shared in the circle group: that they feel happy when their mother says she loves them, when their uncle says they're special, etc.) . . . I notice that Jamie likes it when Mario says . . . (Give more specific examples.)

So words can give happiness. It's almost like giving a flower . . . or sometimes words can hurt like a thorn."

Ask:

- What kinds of words make you feel bad or sad?
- What kinds of words make you angry?
- What kinds of words can you say to others that give happiness?

Say, "Those are some nice things to say. One of the Happiness Points is:"

- ◆ I can give happiness to others with words that are like flowers, not thorns.
- Would anyone like to share about that?

➢ Say, "This week, I'd like us all to pay special attention to giving flowers. If someone does say something mean, you can just say, 'Give me flowers, not thorns.'"

➢ Ask the children to repeat the phrase several times.

➢ The adult can reinforce this, encouraging children to use this as a verbal skill, rather than hitting or saying something mean when others say something negative.

Activity Options

Three to Five Activity: Provide the opportunity for the children to make flowers out of colored paper or paper and colors, or if flowers are plentiful, allow them to go outside and each pick a flower. Then invite them to mill around the room, thinking of words that give happiness. When you give a signal, each child can pair up with the child closest to him or her and exchange their flowers and words of happiness.

Six to Seven Activity: Ask the children to draw or paint a picture about the lesson today. Some children may wish to draw a time when they felt bad, or paint their feelings, while others may draw about feeling happy. Allow them to draw whatever they wish.

Close with a Quietly Being Exercise.

HAPPINESS LESSON 6
The Heart School

The Bear took four cards from the HAPPY box and read them to Marc. *"Be patient, say only kind words, help others, and always have good thoughts about yourself and others."*

"Is this the secret of being happy?" Marc asked.

"Yes," explained the Bear, "and when you are happy, that is when you are the real you! That is why it is so easy to change. "I'll help you!" he added, seeing the look on Marc's face.

"Listen very carefully now," said the Golden Bear. "Tomorrow, when you pack your school bag, open the HAPPY box and take out one card. Read the message carefully, and when you're in school, just do what the card says. If you follow it, it will work! I'll see you tomorrow evening to hear how your day went."

And swiftly the Golden Bear lifted off and floated away with his rainbow-balloon, waving and smiling as Marc waved and smiled back.

The next morning, Marc got out of bed early and got ready quickly. This was going to be the first day of happiness at school. When everything was ready, Marc took a card out of his HAPPY box. As he was taking the first card, it seemed that he could hear the voice of the Golden Bear. "What have you picked Marc? Tell me."

Astonished, Marc looked around but could not see the little Bear. "Strange" he thought, but he really had heard his voice. "Tell me what you have picked," Marc heard again."

"Okay, I took a card and it says, *'Do everything with a* smile.'" Marc said out loud.

"Oh, that is wonderful," Marc could hear the Bear saying. "It is easy! Tell me, what are you going to do?"

Marc started slowly, "I will . . . I will . . . I will say good morning to everyone with a smile. If someone is unfriendly, I will smile instead of hitting him or saying something mean. If my teacher tells me to write neater, I will smile at her instead of getting upset, and . . . " he finished in a rush, "anyway, I will do everything with a smile today."

"Okay," smiled the Golden Bear, "see you this evening!"

When Marc came home from school that day, he could hardly wait to see the little Bear to share all the news with him. Marc looked around and soon the Bear appeared, floating down on his rainbow-balloon.

"I could see your happy face from afar," the Bear said lovingly.

"Yes, Bear, oh, it was a wonderful day! I did everything exactly as I told you this morning and guess what? Not only did I smile," Marc said proudly, "but others started to smile too and seemed to get on better with each other."

"Well done!" said the Bear.

"Yes," added Marc. "And, Hugo wanted to kick me. But I just stood there fearlessly and smiled . . . and you know what happened then? He forgot about kicking me! He sort of looked at me in a funny way and turned around and walked away. I think he forgot about kicking altogether today. It is amazing!" exclaimed Marc. "Oh, I am looking forward to taking another card from the HAPPY box tomorrow. Will you come tomorrow to hear about my happy day?"

"Yes, I will come! Good luck for tomorrow, and be strong!" said the Bear. As the Golden Bear was flying off with his balloon, Marc ended the day happily. Oh, how exciting life can be when you discover something new!

The next morning, Marc got up early again and picked his card for the day from the HAPPY box. "Little Bear, can you hear me? Today I've picked, *be patient.* I've thought about what I will do. Shall I tell you?"

> *I will let others go first,*
> *I will not rush to finish my work too quickly,*
> *(I always want to finish first, so that I get praised)*
> *I will help others patiently and will wait happily, when others are speaking,*
> *I will listen carefully to what my teacher is telling me.*

"Oh, I can hardly wait to get to school today!" said Marc.

Marc had a long day at school. His face was not so happy when he got home. He finished his dinner slowly and went to bed early.

"Oh, I almost forgot, the little Golden Bear wanted to come," thought Marc. It was as if the Bear heard his thoughts, for he was suddenly standing right in front of him.

"It wasn't so easy today, was it?" gently asked the Bear, looking at Marc's face.

"Well, do you know what happened? I did everything as I said this morning, but I forgot one thing, and that was to be patient with myself," said Marc. "I rushed to finish quickly, and because of that, I dropped some paint and it splashed all over the floor! And only then did I remember that I wanted to be patient with myself. Bear, it wasn't pleasant at all! You know why? Not only did I drop the paint, but when one of my classmates started to laugh at me and made fun of me, I said some hurtful words to him. And then I felt awful afterwards."

"Cheer up, Marc! You've only just started to become the happier you! That needs a little time, and these things happen sometimes. Just try not to make the same mistake again," the Bear said in his most encouraging manner.

"I'm glad to hear that, Bear. It makes me feel a lot better!" said Marc.

With a big smile the Bear opened the UNHAPPY box and turned to Marc saying, "Write down your unhappiness about the spilled paint and about being angry with your classmate, and slip it into the UNHAPPY box. Then close the box, and it is over and done with! As easy as that! What's past is past. There's no need to worry or to be upset about it! Try to understand what went wrong, tell yourself that you won't make the same mistake again, and then forget it completely. Remember only what went right today and what made you happy, and think about what you are going to do tomorrow to be happy!" The Golden Bear paused a moment, and then he added, "Tomorrow you will try again and you will succeed, and that's a promise! You are loving and very special, Marc!"

Marc suddenly felt so light and full of confidence. "Yes, tomorrow I will try again and succeed! Oh, I can hardly wait until tomorrow to take the next card!" Marc laughed happily as the Bear grabbed the string of his rainbow-balloon and got ready to float away. The Bear looked at him. His eyes where full of love and hope. Suddenly, Marc felt that his heart too was filling with love and hope. He could feel the great confidence the Bear had in him. "He believes in me and I know it will work! With the help of the little Bear I will be victorious and become the real me, happy and loving!"

Dear children, now that you have just listened to this story, how do you think it will end? Share your ideas with others in your class or with your family.

Note to Educator: Please invite the children to share their ideas about how the story with end.

Okay, listen now to what happened. Day by day, Marc would take a card from his HAPPY box and think about how to use it at school. Most of the time he was good and successful, but sometimes he would make a mistake. When he made a mistake, he would not get upset or worry. Instead, he would try to understand what went wrong, write it on a piece of paper, and tell himself he will not let the same mistake happen again. Then he would slip the paper into the UNHAPPY box and close the lid and forget about it!

And so, day by day Marc grew stronger and stronger and happier and happier. The amazing thing was that after a while, the other children in the class changed too, because he was such a good example to them and his growing happiness worked like magic! Do you want to know what happened in the end?

Gradually all the children in the class discovered the secret about the HAPPY box and asked every day, "Marc, what are you doing today to become happier?"

Marc would share with them what was written on the card. Do you know what happened next? They joined in. In a short time all the children were becoming happier and happier until in the end all the children in the class were treating each other like friends and being loving and caring for each other.

It was such a joy to see this happen!

It was just like magic!

Discuss

- What does patience mean?
- How can we be patient with ourselves?
- How do we feel when others are not patient with us?
- How can we be patient with others?

Activity

Three to Four Activity: Ask the children what they think the Golden Bear would say to them. Perhaps they can all share one thing they think the Golden Bear would say — and then walk around and say those things to each other.

Five to Seven Activity: Ask the children what they would like the Golden Bear to say to them and what they would like to tell the Golden Bear. Ask them to draw a picture of that and write their sentences below their drawing. Invite them to share.

Close with the Peaceful Star Quietly Being Exercise.

HAPPINESS LESSON 8
Happy Boxes

Begin with the Rainbow Song.

Discuss

Talk about the story, and about all the things Marc did that helped him be happier. Then ask the children if they can think of things that would make them happier in class.

Write the suggestions down on a large sheet of paper and discuss them. For young children, draw a symbol next to the suggestion.

Planning Actions: Talk about all the suggestions from the former lesson's discussion. Focus your attention on the practical suggestions. Choosing one at a time, think and share your ideas about them, and then make a plan of how to put the ideas into action. Success is easily achieved if the whole class or group works on the same plan. That creates enthusiasm and a sense of unity.

Activity

The teacher can decide whether he or she wants the children to make individual Happy Boxes, or one Happy Box for the class. Help the children write their ideas for happiness on little slips of paper that go into the box or for children ages three and four write their ideas as they contribute them verbally.

Begin making the boxes.

Close with a Quietly Being Exercise.

HAPPINESS LESSON 9
Cards for the Happy Boxes

Begin with the Rainbow song.

Activity

Finish making the Happy and Unhappy Boxes and decorate them.

Discuss: In "The Heart School Story," Marc learns that it is important not to get upset with himself or anyone else.

Ask:

- What did Marc learn to do? (To sit together, reflect briefly on what went wrong, and then focus attention on progress and not on mistakes made.)
- Shall we do that, too?

Activity

Ask the children to write cards for the Happy Box, putting a practical suggestion that would make them happier on each card. Help them as needed. You may want to put one-word suggestions for the youngest children, perhaps adding a little picture. Put them into the Happy Box.

Arrange for each child to select one card from the Happy Box — if it is a Happy Box for the whole class — or one child from each group if there are several boxes. Share ideas within your group or class, and make an action plan together in order to achieve what is written on the card.

Close with a Quietly Being Exercise.

Note to Educator: You may wish to keep the Happy and Unhappy Boxes for your class if the children like them and appear to benefit. Either daily or weekly, take one card out of the box. Try this for at least four weeks. At least once a week share your experiences and progress with each other, and also look for areas that need improvement. As the children discover new ways to be happy, ask them to write those down on new cards.

HAPPINESS LESSON 10
Giving Happiness

Begin with a song.

Share a Story

Three and Four Story: Ready the story, "What shall I give to Nini?" by Tea Lobjanidze. It is Item 3 in the Appendix.

Five to Seven Story: Read the story, "Billy the Bully," by John McConnel. It is Item 4 in the Appendix.

Discuss the following Happiness Point in relation to the story:

♦ When I do good things, I am happy with myself.

Ask:

• What good things do you do that make you happy with yourself?
• What good things do you do at school?
• What good things do you do at home?
• What good things do you do for the world?

List the things the children say on the board.

Activity

Invite the children to draw a picture about the good things they do.
Close with a Quietly Being Exercise.

HAPPINESS LESSON 11
Sharing

Begin with a song.

Discuss/Share

Say, "Today we're going to talk about sharing. Every day we share things at school — we share our smiles, and we share tables, and crayons and scissors."

Ask:

- What else do we share?
- When do you like to share?
- Is it hard to share sometimes? When? (Affirm their responses, such as, "Yes, sometimes it's hard to share our very favorite thing.")
- When is it easy to share?

Discuss the following Happiness Point:

♦ I can give happiness to others by sharing.

Then ask the children what they would like to share. Perhaps they would like to:

❖ practice sharing during playtime
❖ think about another way to share the toys
❖ bring something to share from home, or
❖ make something in class they can share such as sweets or cards.

Keep in mind that many children are not ready to share developmentally until they are four or five years old. The teacher can make the sharing easy by having enough of the same things (such as crackers).

Activity

Practice sharing with happiness: Set up a situation for sharing inside or outside. Tell the children that you want them to practice sharing with happiness. When you sound the bell, you want them to go to the child closest to them and offer to share what they are using, playing with, etc. Ring the bell at least three times!

Close with a Quietly Being Exercise.

HAPPINESS LESSON 12

Good Wishes

Begin with a song.

Discuss/Share

Say, "A secret that hardly anyone knows is that it's easy to be happy if you have good wishes for everyone."

Discuss two Happiness Points:

- ◆ Good wishes for everyone make me happy inside.
- ◆ I can give happiness to everyone with my good wishes.

Ask:

- • What does that mean?
- • Can anyone tell us about a time when everyone had good wishes for you?
- • What did that feel like?
- • How do we give happiness to others with our good wishes?

➤ Say, "Let's fill ourselves up with love like we did last week." Begin the Filling Up with Love Quietly Being Exercise.

➤ Say, "Now, I want you to walk around the room and look at everyone with good wishes. . . . Isn't that easy? How does that feel? . . . Okay, let's end with a happy song."

Sing the following song or another song on happiness from your culture.

Song: The Happy Stars

^GI am happy, I am happy,

I am a ^{D7}star,

I am happy, I am happy,

I am a star.

I am happy to remember

to ^Csparkle forever,

I am ^Ghappy, I am ^{D7}happy,

I am a ^Gstar.

I give my love to ^Geveryone,

I give it ^{D7}from my heart.

I ^Ggive my sparkle to everyone,

and ^{D7}make them sparkle too.

(Repeat first verse)

Activity

Invite the children to use finger paints to make a picture of happiness or the feelings of happiness.

Close with a Quietly Being Exercise.

HAPPINESS LESSON 13
Making Washing Lines of Happiness

Begin with a happy song.

Activity

Step 1. Draw happy faces on paper using chalk, pencil, crayon, pastel.

Step 2. Cut the faces into lovely shapes of all different shapes and sizes.

Step 3. Hang the happy faces on a washing line inside the school or outside.

Reflection: Enjoy seeing happy faces.

Remember to remember that your face is the best face to show happiness.

Smile and you will spread sunshine through your smile.

Share your happiness and tell if someone is hurting you.

— *Contributed by Hadeel Jarrar*

Close with a Quietly Being Exercise of your choice.

HAPPINESS LESSON 14
Happy Star Dance

Begin with a song.

Share: Invite each child to share his or her finger painting. Place them on the wall in the form of a star.

Sing the Happy Star song again.

Dance: Once the children know the Happy Star song and can sing it from memory, they can dance to it as well. You may wish to do the movements below, or a simpler version.

Dance Movement 1. Children skip around in a circle facing inwards.

Dance Movement 2. Turn outwards when singing the first "star" and skip in the opposite direction.

Dance Movement 3. Crouch down when singing the second "star," then rise slowly bringing their arms up over their heads.

Dance Movement 4. Continue to skip around, stopping on "star" and turning to face inwards again.

Share a Story: The Seed

Once upon a time there was a boy named Juan. He was six-years old and lived in a small house next to a river at the foot of a mountain with his parents and a sister a little older than he. One day, when coming back from school, he heard a voice that cried, "Help, help! Please, help me!"

Juan listened and searched until at last he was standing in a spot where the voice seemed loudest. He looked around but could not see anybody. The voice said, "Look down. I'm here." Much to his surprise, the voice seemed to be coming from a brown seed about the size of his thumb. This seed was lying on a stone.

Juan asked, "What's wrong?" A sad voice came from the seed and said, "I am so glad you came along. I have been sitting and sitting on this stone for ever so long. Several other people came by, but they did not stop. I was afraid no one would stop."

"Why, I'm surprised they didn't stop!" said Juan. "Sometimes people get so busy they forget to listen," he explained politely.

The seed said, "I've been sitting here for a long time. I know there is something I must do, something I must know. But I'm not sure what it is. Do you know my purpose?"

Johnny was surprised at such a question. He looked at the seed very carefully and slowly said, "Well, I understand why you are sad if you do not know your purpose. That is very important. But, don't worry! I will take you with me and I will look for the right place for you to live. I will try and help you figure out what you need. Then you will discover by yourself, little by little, your purpose. I do know that everyone can give something important to the world. I bet you can, too."

And that is how Johnny found the seed the size of his thumb and ended up taking it home. When he arrived home, he talked to his mother, and she told him what seeds need. The next morning, he made a hole on the sunny side of the house. He carefully loosened the soil and gently placed the brown seed inside. Then he covered the hole with soil and watered it.

But the following day, the seed began to cry again, saying, "Help! I am alone again and everything is dark! Why has Johnny left me here?"

When Johnny heard the seed crying, he apologized for forgetting to explain why he did what he did. Then Johnny said, "Don't worry and don't feel sad, it is necessary that you have some time to prepare for what you need to do. I will come to visit you every day, and I will take care of you. I will give you water every day, and you will see that in a little time, you will grow. Be happy inside and know that you are preparing to serve.

Soon you will notice that you are growing little roots. And soon a stem will start to grow upward. That will be called your trunk."

Then the seed asked the boy, "Did you also have to take time to prepare?"

"Of course," answered Johnny, "Everyone has to prepare — that's part of being responsible. Now I am preparing at school. I know I'm smart and I know how to think and learn. Be patient. It takes time to prepare, and everything prepares in its own way."

Just as Johnny had said, he came to visit the seed and give it water every day. The seed grew and grew. Soon a stem started to peek through the ground, and two little leaves began to unfold. The sun warmed it and gave it light. It grew stronger and taller, and it became apparent that the seed was growing into a strong, wonderful tree!

The boy and the tree continued to talk. After several years, flowers began to blossom all over the tree, and little green balls grew from them. These changed in color from green to blush and finally to exactly the color of apricots.

The now larger boy carefully picked the first ripe apricots and praised the tree. "You have grown into a strong apricot tree, and your apricots are delicious."

So this small seed, with the care of a boy who knew how to be responsible, became something very important. The tree said to Johnny, "Thank you, friend, for taking care of me with so much love. Now I know my purpose!"

Juan answered, "You are very, very important. As a tree you give us clean air, shade, beauty, and even fruit to eat. I am your friend, but you are a friend to the whole world."

And that's how this tale ends.

Ask:

- How was Juan responsible in the story? How did he help the seed?
- What was the seed's purpose?
- The seed was preparing to be a tree and give apricots by growing roots in the ground. How was Juan preparing?
- Juan said it take time to prepare. In school when you learn and study you are preparing. What are you preparing for?
- Do you know like Juan that you are smart?
- Are you patient with yourself and others like Juan?
- What are you responsible for?
- What would you like to be responsible for?

Activity

Three to Five Activity: Play pretend with the things the children say they would like to be responsible for. Facilitate those who wish to be responsible for one thing to act that out that role, pretend helping the other children. Then allow the other children to act out another role.

Six and Seven Activity: Invite the children to draw a picture of what they would like to be responsible for and share that with others.

RESPONSIBILITY LESSON 6

Trying My Best

Introduce: "Sometimes people stop being responsible because they think something is hard and they can't do it. But everyone has things that are hard for them to do. When you were much smaller you could not do the things you can do now. As you get bigger, you will be able to do even more things.

Let's listen to a song about that!

Note to Educator: The following song can be downloaded on the LVE international website under For Schools/Children Ages 3–7/Download Songs.

Share a Song: I'll Try

What if a baby said, "I can't crawl."
Or a monkey, "I can't climb."
A morning dove, "I can't sing."
And they said, "I can't" to everything?

The baby would get fat and bored.
The monkey sit and stare.
The morning dove, would feel left out,
And they'd say, "I don't care."
But, what if instead they said:

Chorus: "I'll try. I won't give up the ship.
Thought I may fall down, I'll get right up.
I really, really, really, will try."

The baby learned to crawl.
And the monkey learned to climb. Hip, Hip.
The morning dove sang this song.
And he wants you to sing along.

(Repeat chorus two times.)

— *Contributed by Madeline C. Nella*

Discuss/Share

Ask:

- What are your responsibilities at school?
- How do you feel when you do a good job?
- What do you say to yourself then?
- How do you feel about learning something new?
- How do you feel when something is hard?

UNIT EIGHT: SIMPLICITY AND CARING FOR THE EARTH AND HER OCEANS

Simplicity and Caring for the Earth and Her Oceans Lessons

Caring for the Earth and Her Oceans has been added to this updated Simplicity Unit, as simplicity is a value that allows us to recognize the beauty and importance of nature and our animal friends, and honor our planet. The six Living Green Values lessons for children ages three through seven, drawn from *Living Green Values Activities for Children and Young Adults, A Special Rio+20 Edition*, are included in this unit.

These lessons are intended to help children be more aware of the importance of taking care of the Earth and her resources. Part of that process is awakening love for nature and her creatures and learning about specific ways that they can help be a friend to the Earth. Enjoy doing the activities with the children. Thank you for helping take care of our Earth — and the children. If you wish, send us your comments and news about their activities!

Simplicity Reflection Points are used to help define the value. The points can be used as the first focus point during values time, or can be a discussion point as part of language arts. Allow the children the opportunity to share their experiences about that value.

For five- through seven-year olds, the teacher can choose to use some of the words and sentences as content for reading, spelling, and writing. As the students continue with the unit, they can create their own Simplicity Points. They can then draw or write those, or make up short stories.

Simplicity and Caring for Our Earth and Her Oceans Reflection Points

- ♦ Simplicity is enjoying simple things.
- ♦ Simplicity is natural.
- ♦ Simplicity is learning from the earth.
- ♦ Simplicity is beautiful.

♦ Simplicity is using what we already have.

♦ Caring for Our Earth and Her Oceans is important.

♦ Our Earth is our home and the home of animals.

♦ Nature is beautiful.

♦ We can all be Friends of the Earth by not littering.

♦ We can all be Friends of the Earth by not wasting.

Simplicity and Caring for Our Earth and Her Oceans Unit Goals and Objectives

Goal: To increase understanding about simplicity and appreciation of nature, birds and animals.

Objectives:

❑ To identify simple pleasures and simple things they enjoy.

❑ To enjoy playing with simple things.

❑ To think and be involved in a discussion about the things trees provide for humans and animals.

❑ To learn about where water comes from and to enjoy acting out that process.

❑ To be engaged in stories to develop more love for birds.

❑ To learn about how seeds grow into plants.

Goal: To learn a few ways to help take care of the Earth and animals.

Objectives:

❑ To hear that trees give oxygen to humans and animals; to understand that trees are important and to participate in cooperatively planting a tree.

❑ To discuss the many ways water is important and to learn about the importance of not wasting water.

❑ To understand how birds and animals can be hurt by people's trash and plastic.

❑ To learn about the importance of not littering and reusing or limiting the use of plastic and be motivated by the activities to not litter and help care for the Earth.

❑ To plant flower or vegetable seeds and care for the plants as they grow.

❑ To send love and peace to birds, animals and the Earth and Her Oceans by engaging in Quietly Being Exercises.

❑ To understand that conservation is using what we have and not wasting.

❑ To practice conservation as part of class projects, for example, using the other side of a piece of paper and recycling paper.

❑ To make their own learning materials as part of one activity.

❑ To decide as a group to do one or two things to help nature, and to carry through on the ideas.

SIMPLICITY LESSON 1
Simple Pleasures

Begin with a song.

Introduce: "In the next few weeks we are going to learn about simplicity. Simplicity means valuing what is natural, what is simple. We will also learn about valuing our earth and her oceans. Today, I want you to think of things that are simple, things that are natural, things that you don't have to buy. For example, a simple pleasure in life is enjoying a pretty flower, or getting a hug from someone who loves you."

Discuss/Share

Some of the Simplicity Points are:

♦ Simplicity is natural.

♦ Simplicity is enjoying simple things.

Ask:

• What simple pleasures do you enjoy? (Perhaps singing, being read a story.)

• What are simple things you enjoy doing? (Help the children think of things they enjoy in their location, such as making throwing snowballs or making sand castles.)

• What simple things do you like to play with? (Please help them think of things they can play with in their location, such as making a fort out of discarded boxes, toys out of bamboo or puppets out of sticks.)

• What is a simple game you can play that doesn't need anything you have to buy?

Activity

Play something simple, that doesn't require buying anything or using anything mechanical. This could be enjoying a walk outdoors, lying on the ground outside and enjoying the clouds or the trees, playing a game, dancing together, etc.

Close with a Quietly Being Exercise if it wasn't part of your activity.

"Shhhhh," said the Blue Heron in his deep voice, "you'll attract attention."

All the birds instantly stopped.

"You tell them, little Tern," said the Blue Heron, nodding encouragingly.

"Okay," said the little Tern with a little chirp. "Our Earth and the animals are getting sick because the humans have forgotten about love and respect for each other, and us, and the Earth. Maybe it'll be easier if I say it in a poem (or a song) …?"

(Song: The Tern's Song)

Be friends with each other,

Be loving and sweet,

To girls and boys and all you meet!

Be friends to the birds, the cats and the dogs,

The horses, the geese, the goats and the frogs,

Pick up your trash. . . .

Don't pollute the water,

Don't waste things please,

Don't poison the ground,

the water, sky or trees . . .

Pick up your trash. . . .

Be a friend to each other,

All countries and groups,

Love and respect us animals,

And the Earth, too.

Recycle, don't waste,

Pick up your trash….

Humans are powerful and smart,

But learn to be kind,

Then we'll all live safely,

And have a wonderful glorious time!

The colors of the Earth will sparkle,

The meadows and flowers will bloom,

We birds will sing happily then,

And not be in a state of gloom!

Rosa and David applauded and the birds all flapped their wings in approval. Well, all but the Blue Heron.

He said in his deep voice, "Well done, little Tern." All the birds became very quiet. They all looked solemnly at Rosa and David and seemed to be waiting.

"I promise to help," said Rosa.

"Me too," said David.

Discuss

Ask the following questions, acknowledging their answers.

- Were Rosa and David surprised that the birds talked to them?
- Why did the birds want to talk to Rosa and David?
- How were the birds getting hurt?
- Have you ever seen a bird that was hurt?
- What can we do to help the birds?

Say, "Let's listen to the little Tern's poem (song) again." Please read the poem or sing it as a song.

Ask:

- What does respect mean?
- How can we respect each other?
- How can we respect all animals?
- How can we respect the Earth?
- What can you do to help the Earth?
- What can we do in our classroom?
- What can you do at your home?
- What can we do on the playground?

Help the children come up with practical ideas that they can do to be a Friend of the Earth. Write down the ideas in a simple way, perhaps using pictures as symbols. Select a couple that you can do in your class.

Activity

Implement one of the ideas. For example, if you don't yet have a trash can, trash box or place for recycling materials, perhaps now would be a good time to set one up. Children can also recycle sheets of paper by using the other side.

Begin an ecological organic gardening project with the children (or another ecological project). Perhaps plant seeds in a small garden or plant seeds in individual cups. Talk about how we can help our Earth by not littering and not putting poisons on the ground.

Close with the Quietly Being Exercise, Sending Love to the Birds and Animals.

SIMPLICITY LESSON 5
Being a Friend of the Earth

Begin with a song. Please choose a song about peace, love, respect or caring for the earth or sing the poem of the Tern in the last lesson.

Share a Story: Rosa and David Help the Earth

Rosa and David waved goodbye to the birds and ran all the way home.

"Mama, mama!" they called out of breath when they opened the front door. Their words tumbled out as they told her what had happened.

Mama looked at them with surprise when they told her the story, then she looked puzzled. She sat silently for a while as though she was really thinking before asking, "Can you tell me the poem (song) again?"

Rosa and David tried to remember it all.

215

Talk about conservation. "Conservation means we don't waste what nature gives us. We plant one or two trees when we use one, and we re-use the resources they give.

Ask:

- How can we conserve the things that come from trees in the classroom? (paper, boxes, sticks)
- What kinds of things do people waste sometimes?
- What are other ways you can conserve?
- ➢ With your guidance, help the children pick one or two things you can do in the classroom to conserve.

Creative Activity

Make up a song or poem about conservation. The following poem points out that one way of conserving is not needing to have one of everything!

> It's okay to be simple,
> It's okay to be kind.
> I love the earth —
> I don't need
> one of every kind!

If you are in a community where the children have an abundance of things, perhaps talk to the parents and children about "recycling" some things to those in need.

Close with Sending Love to the Birds and Animals, A Quietly Being Exercise.

SIMPLICITY LESSON 10
Making Our Own Learning Material

Begin with a song.

Awareness: We can create our own learning material in a simple way.

Activity

Ask the children to create their own number or alphabet books.

Three and Four Activity: The teacher will need to trace the numbers 1 through 5 or 1 through 10, each number on a separate piece of paper. The children can then put the corresponding number of happy faces or flowers or stars on those sheets of paper.

Five through Seven Activity: Think about what the children need or want to learn and create the opportunity for them to make a little booklet or visual aid. Or, small groups of children can create a poster. Perhaps some would like to learn the name of trees. They could put leaves on a paper with the name of the tree or label different pine cones, etc.

Close with one of the Quietly Being Exercises.

SIMPLICITY LESSON 11
Making Our Playthings

Begin with a song. Perhaps use objects found in nature to make music to go with your song.

Awareness: When we play with simple things, we can be creative and use our imagination. We are also recycling by using those things again.

Activity

Place before the children during playtime cardboard boxes collected from the grocery store or fruit stand or other types of containers that are available free of charge. Children at ages three and four will often start playing spontaneously with the boxes, sometimes two or three squeezing inside one box and using another box as a lid, saying "This is our house." Or, they can pretend it is a train and sing, "The wheels on the train go round and round." They can make a tower, etc.

Close with a Quietly Being Exercise of your choice.

SIMPLICITY LESSON 12
Planting Trees

Preparation: Let the children prepare by collecting containers for water, small spades, pieces of paper, saplings and so on.

Sing a song about the beauty of trees or nature.

Discuss

Tell the children that we need to help the environment by planting trees.

Say, "Trees help human beings as when we breathe out, the trees take our old air and make oxygen so we can breathe new air. Trees also help the Earth in other ways. They